An Indian winter

An Indian winter

OR

With the Indians in the Rockies

JAMES WILLARD SCHULTZ

**WITH A FRONTISPIECE BY
GEORGE VARIAN**

GYAN

Published by

GYAN

Gyan Publishing House
5, Ansari Road
Daryaganj, New Delhi-110002
Phone: 011-47034999, 9811692060
E-mail: books@gyanbooks.com

Distribution Network
gyanbooks.com
India, USA, Canada, UK, Australia, France

ISBN: 978-81-212-8929-0 (PB)
First Published, 1913

2nd Impression 2023

Printed at: Gyan Press, Delhi.

AN INDIAN WINTER

AUTHOR: JAMES WILLARD SCHULTZ

An Indian Winter

OR

With the Indians in the Rockies

BY

JAMES WILLARD SCHULTZ

WITH A FRONTISPIECE BY
GEORGE VARIAN

BOSTON AND NEW YORK
HOUGHTON MIFFLIN COMPANY
The Riverside Press Cambridge
1913

Published September 1912

THIS BOOK IS AFFECTIONATELY DEDICATED

TO MY WIFE

CELIA HAWKINS SCHULTZ

WHOSE GOOD COMRADESHIP AND SYMPATHY

HAVE BEEN MY GREATEST HELP

IN WRITING THE TALE

Preface

WHEN in the seventies I turned my back on civilization and joined the trappers and traders of the Northwest, Thomas Fox became my friend. We were together in the Indian camps and trading posts often for months at a time; he loved to recount his adventures in still earlier days, and thus it was that I learned the facts of his life. The stories that he told by the evening camp-fire and before the comfortable fireplaces of our various posts, on long winter days, were impressed upon my memory, but to make sure of them I frequently took notes of the more important points.

As time passed, I realized more and more how unusual and interesting his adventures were, and I urged him to write an account of them. He began with enthusiasm, but soon tired of the unaccustomed work. Later, however, after the buffalo had been exterminated and we were settled on a cattle-ranch, where the life was of a deadly monotony compared with that which we had led, I induced him to take up the narrative once more. Some parts of it he wrote with infinite detail; other parts consisted only of dates and a few sentences.

He was destined never to finish the task. An old bullet wound in his lung had always kept him in poor health, and when, in the winter of 1885, he contracted pneumonia, the end was quick. His last request was that I would put his notes in shape for publication. This I have done to the best of my ability in my own old age; how well I have done it is for the reader to judge.

Brave, honest old Ah-ta-to-yi (The Fox), as the Blackfeet and frontiers-men loved to call him! We buried him on a high bluff overlooking the valley of the Two Medicine River, and close up to the foothills of the Rockies, the "backbone-of-the-world" that he loved so well. After we had filled in the grave and the others had gone, Pitamakan and I sat by the new-made mound until the setting sun and the increasing cold warned us also to descend into the valley. The old chief was crying as we mounted our horses.

"Although of white skin," he faltered, "the man who lies there was my brother. I doubt not that I shall soon meet him in the Sand-hills."

AH-PUN-I LODGE,
February, 1912.

With the Indians in the Rockies

CHAPTER I

MY father kept a little firearm shop in St. Louis. Over it was the sign:—

DAVID FOX & Co.
Wholesale & Retail Guns
& Ammunition.
Fine Rifles & Fowling Pieces
Made To Order.

"Co." on the sign stood for my uncle, Wesley Fox, who was a silent partner in the business. Longer than I could remember, he had been an employee of the American Fur Company away up the Missouri River.

It was a great event in the quiet life of our little family of three when he came, as he did every two or three years, to pay us a short visit. He no sooner set foot in the house than my mother began to cook bread, cakes, puddings and pies. I have seen him make what he called a delicious breakfast on nothing but buttered toast and coffee. That was because he did not get any bread where he lived except on Christmas Day. Every pound of freight that went up the river above Fort Union in the company's keel-boats and bateaux was for the Indian trade, and there was no room for such luxuries as flour.

While Uncle Wesley was with us, mother always let me put away my books, and not say any lessons to her, and I went with him everywhere in the town. That is what St. Louis was in those days—just a good-sized town. I liked best to go with him to the levee and see the trappers and traders coming in, their bateaux loaded down with beaver and other fur pelts. Nearly all these men wore buckskin clothes and moccasins, and fur caps of their own make. They all had long hair and big whiskers and mustaches that looked as if they had been trimmed with a butcher-knife.

Every time my Uncle Wesley came out of the Far West he brought me a bow and arrows in a fine case and quiver; or a stone-headed war-club; real weapons that had killed buffalo and been in battles between the tribes. And once he brought me a Sioux scalp, the heavy braided hair all of four feet in length. When I asked him where he got it he laughed a little and said, "Oh, I got it up there near Fort Union." But I had seen my mother shake her head at him, and by that I knew that I was not to be told more. I guessed, though, that he had taken that scalp himself, and long afterward I found out that I had guessed right.

One night I heard the family talking about me. I had been sent to bed and was supposed to be asleep, but as the door to my room was open and I was lying wide awake,

I could n't help hearing. My mother was taking Uncle Wesley to task. "You know that the presents you bring him only add to his interest in trapping and trading," she said, "and as it is, we don't succeed very well in interesting him in his studies, and in the life we have planned for him."

"You know how our hearts are set on his going to Princeton," said my father, in his always low, gentle voice, "and then becoming such a preacher as his grandfather was before him. You must help us, Wesley. Show the boy the dark side of the plains life, the hardships and dangers of it."

In our little sitting-room there was a picture of Grandfather Fox, a tall, dark man with a long wig. He wore a long-tailed coat with a tremendous collar, knee-breeches, black stockings, and shoes with enormous buckles. I thought that I should not like to be a preacher if that was the way I must dress. And thinking that, I lost the rest of what they were saying and fell asleep.

Uncle Wesley stayed with us only a few days that spring. He intended to remain a month, but one morning Pierre Chouteau, the head of the great fur company, came to our house and had a long talk with him, with the result that he left for Fort Union the very next day, to take the place of some one who had died there.

So I went back to my studies, and my parents kept me closer at home than ever. I was allowed to go out on real play spells only for two hours on Saturday afternoons. There were very few American boys in the town in those days. Most of my playmates were French Creoles, who spoke very little English, or none at all, so naturally I learned their patois. That knowledge was very useful to me in after days.

I am going to pass over what I have to say now as quickly as possible, for even after all these years, and old as I am, the thought of it still hurts. In February of the following winter my father fell ill of smallpox and died. Then my mother and I took it, and my mother died also.

I did not know anything about her death until many days after she was buried, and then I wanted to die, too. I felt that there was nothing in the world for me, until one day Pierre Chouteau himself came for me in his grand carriage, took me to his house, and kept me there until May, when my uncle arrived again in St. Louis.

Uncle Wesley put on what we call "a bold front" when he came to me, but for all that I could see that he was very sad. We had just one talk about my future. "I should like to carry out your father's and mother's plans for you, Tom," he said. "The only way to do it, so far as I can see, is to send you to Cynthia Mayhew, in Hartford, Connecticut. She loved your mother, — they were just like sisters, — and I know that she would be glad to take care of you and see to your education."

I broke out crying, and said that if he

sent me away from him I should die. How could he be so cruel as to send me far away among strangers? And then I cried all the harder, although I was ashamed of myself for doing so.

Uncle Wesley almost broke down himself. He gulped hard two or three times, and his voice was n't steady as he took me on his lap and felt of my spindling legs and arms.

"Poor boy! You are weak," he said. "Weak in body and low in mind. Well, we 'll say no more about this matter of your education now. I 'll take you up the river with me for a year, or until you get good and strong. But we 'll pack your study books along, and a good part of your mother's library, and you 'll have to dig into them every evening after we get settled. Now that 's fair, is n't it?"

It was more than fair. My fondest dream was to be realized. I was actually to see the country and the Indians and the great herds of buffalo. There was nothing in St. Louis now to keep my uncle or make his stay there a pleasure. As quickly as possible he disposed of the little shop and its contents, and deposited the entire proceeds with the company for me "for a rainy day," as he said.

On April 10, 1856, we left St. Louis on the Chippewa, a fine new boat that the company had just bought. I was thirteen years old, and that was my first steamboat ride. As the stern-wheel craft swung out from the levee and steamed rapidly — as it seemed to me — up-stream, the novel experience gave me the keenest pleasure. I fairly hugged myself as I remembered that by the channel of the river it was more than two thousand miles to our destination.

We no sooner left the Mississippi and turned into the more muddy waters of the Missouri than I earnestly begged my uncle to get his rifle out of the cabin and load it, so as to be ready to shoot buffalo. I was terribly disappointed when he told me that many days must pass before we should see any of the animals. But to please me he brought the rifle to the cabin deck and fired a couple of shots at the sawyers in the river. Again he loaded the piece, and told me to shoot at one.

"Even boys must know how to shoot where we are going," he said. "Now take a fine sight at the end of that little sawyer and let's see how near it you can place a bullet."

I did as I was told and fired, after a long, wabbly aim; the water splashed just over the tip of the log, and a number of passengers clapped their hands and praised me.

That shot began my training in shooting. Every day after that, until we got to the game country, I spent an hour shooting at different objects in the water and on the banks. One morning I fired at one of a pair of wild geese. The bird gave a flap or two of its great wings, its head dropped, and it floated inertly with the current.

"I killed it!" I shouted. "I killed it! Wasn't that a fine shot, uncle?"

He was silent a moment, and then said gravely:—

"It was a thoughtless boy's shot. And I hope it will be the only one. A true hunter never takes the life of God's creatures needlessly."

That was all he said, but the reproof was enough. I took it to heart, and all my life I have not only profited by it, but preached to others against the wanton taking of life.

After passing St. Charles, Missouri, the ranches of the settlers were farther and farther apart, and in a few days we saw the last of them and were in the wild country. Game now became more and more frequent, especially white-tail deer, of which we soon had some for the table. The boat was always tied to an island or to the shore at sundown, and during the short remainder of daylight we would all scatter in the near timber to hunt. A number of wild turkeys were killed, which made us some fine feasts. On these occasions, however, I was only a follower of the hunters. My red-letter day was yet to come.

At Fort Pierre we saw a great number of Sioux Indians. Formerly a company post, it had been sold to the United States, and was now occupied by several companies of soldiers. Two days after leaving the fort, we sighted the first of the buffalo herds, a small band of bulls that splashed out of the river not far ahead of the boat, and took to the hills. About four o'clock that afternoon, the port engine breaking down, we had to make a long stop for repairs. As soon as we swung into the bank and learned that the boat would be tied there for the night, my uncle got out his rifle, and we went hunting.

The timber bordering the river was half a mile wide, with an undergrowth of willow- and rose-brush so thick that we never could have penetrated it but for the game trails crossing it in every direction. From the looks of them, I thought that thousands of animals must be living there. The trails were worn deep by their sharp hoofs.

In places the earth was moist but hard, and there the tracks were plainly outlined. My uncle pointed out the difference in them — how the tracks of the deer differed from those of elk, and how these differed again from the tracks of the buffalo. I was taught, too, that wolf tracks were longer than those of the mountain-lion, which were nearly circular. Finally, I was asked to prove my knowledge.

"What made those tracks?" I was asked.

I hesitated a moment, and replied that I thought buffalo had made them.

"Right," said my uncle. "They seem very fresh; we will follow them."

The myriad tracks of different game, the mystery of the deep woods, the thought that hostile Indians might be there hunting us, all combined to excite me. My heart thumped rapidly and I found it difficult to breathe. I was afraid, and kept looking intently in all directions — even behind me, for I expected every moment to see something come charging through the brush, either to rend us with sharp claws or to stick our bodies full of arrows.

But nothing could have induced me to admit that I felt so; gritting my teeth, I followed on uncertain legs, close at Uncle Wesley's heels. So close was I that when he suddenly stopped, I bumped into him, and then gave a little squeal of fright, for I thought that he had discovered something to justify my fears.

"*Sh-h-h-h!*" he cautioned, and reaching back and drawing me to his side, he pointed significantly ahead.

We were only a few yards from the outer edge of the timber; a hundred yards farther on were three buffalo bulls, standing motionless on the open, sparsely grassed bottom-land. How big they were! How majestic and yet uncouth they loomed before me! They had apparently no necks at all. Forgetting entirely our purpose in coming there, I stared at them with intense interest, until my uncle passed me the rifle and whispered, "Take that farthest one. He is young and in good condition. Aim low, close behind his shoulder."

My hands closed on the long-barreled, heavy weapon. Heretofore my boy strength had been sorely taxed to shoot with it, but now, in my tense excitement, it fairly leaped to my shoulder, and I was able to hold it steady. I pulled the trigger.

Bang! A thick cloud of powder smoke drifted into my face, and then passed on, and I saw two of the bulls running across the bottom; the other was swaying, staggering round and round, with blood streaming from its mouth. Before I could reload, it toppled over with a crash and lay still.

I stood staring at the animal like one in a dream; it was hard to realize that I had actually killed it. Uncle Wesley broke my trance by praising the shot I had made, and added that the animal was in fine condition and would weigh all of a ton. He had me lie down on it, my feet even with its fore feet, and I found that I could not reach the top of its withers, or rather, its hump: its height had been more than six feet.

I now got my first lesson in skinning and butchering one of these great animals. Without axe or windlass, or any of the other things regarded as indispensable by farmers and by professional butchers, the old-time plainsmen made a quick and neat job of this work with only a common butcher-knife.

First, my uncle doubled up the bull's fore legs and straightened back the hind ones. Then, little by little, he twisted the great head sharply back beside the body, at the same time heaving up the back, and in a moment or two the animal lay prone on its belly, propped up in that position by the head. If the skin had been wanted, the rolling-up of the animal would have been reversed, and it would have lain on its back, legs up, and as in the other way, propped in position by the bent-back head.

After making an incision along the back from head to tail, he skinned both sides down to the ground, and even under the body, by propping the head one way and then another, and slanting the carcass so that there was knife room beneath. At last the body lay free, back up, on the clean, spread-out skin.

The choicest part of it was the so-called "hump," or in frontier language, the "boss ribs." These dorsal ribs rose gradually from the centre of the back to a length of twenty inches and more just above the point of the shoulders, and were deeply covered with rich tenderloin.

It took but a moment to get the set off. Uncle Wesley cut an incision along each side at the base of them; then he unjointed a hind leg at the gambrel-joint, and with that for a club he hit the tips of the ribs a few blows, causing them to snap off from the back-bone like so many pipe-stems, and the whole hump lay free on the hide.

Next, he removed the legs with a few deft cuts of the knife, and laid them out on the clean grass; unjointed the backbone at the third rib and removed the after part; severed the neck from the big ribs, cut them apart at the brisket, and smashed one side of them free from the backbone with the leg club, and there we had the great animal divided in eight parts. Lastly, he removed the tongue through an incision in the lower jaw.

"There," said he, when it was all done, "now you know how to butcher. Let's hurry to the boat and get the roustabouts to carry in the meat."

From this point on, there were days at a time when we saw no Indians, and the various kinds of game animals were more and more plentiful and tame. At last, several days after passing Fort Clarke, we came to the American Fur Company's greater post, Fort Union, situated on the north bank of the river about five miles above the mouth of the Yellowstone.

It was begun in 1829, under the direction of the factor, Kenneth McKenzie, and finished in 1832. A stockade of logs ten or twelve feet long, set up on end, side by side, protected the buildings, and this, in turn, was commanded by two-storied bastions, in which cannon were mounted at the northeast and southwest corners.

When we approached the place, a flag was run up on the staff of the fort, cannon boomed a welcome, and a great crowd of Indians and company men, headed by the factor, gathered at the shore to greet us. My uncle and I were escorted to the two-story house which formed the rear of the fort, and in which were the quarters of the factor and clerks.

I learned afterward that distinguished guests had been housed there: George Catlin, the painter and philanthropist, in 1832; Maximilian, Prince of Neuwied, in 1833; and

Audubon, the great naturalist, in 1843. All of them published extremely interesting accounts of what they saw and did in the Upper Missouri country, which I commend to the reader, Maximilian's "Travels in North America" especially; for I went up the river from Fort Union just as he did, and there had been practically no change in the conditions of the country from his time to mine. Maximilian gives a wonderfully accurate and vivid description of the remarkable scenery of the Missouri, without question the most strangely picturesque river in America, and probably in the world.

My Uncle Wesley was a valued clerk of the American Fur Company. He was sent from one to another of their Far Western forts, as occasion for his services arose, and frequently he was in full charge of a post for months at a time, while the factor went on a trip to the States. When we arrived in Fort Union he was told that he must go on to Fort Benton, where the factor needed his help. At that time, since the company's steamboats went no farther than Fort Union, all the goods for the posts beyond were sent in keel-boats, or bateaux. It was not until the summer of 1860 that the extreme upper river was found to be navigable, and on July 2 of that year the Chippewa and the Key West arrived at Fort Benton.

A keel-boat was lying at Fort Union when we arrived there; it was waiting for part of the Chippewa's cargo of ammunition, guns, and various trade goods, mostly tobacco, red and blue cloth, brass wire for jewelry, Chinese vermilion, and small trinkets. These were soon transferred, and we resumed our voyage, Uncle Wesley in charge of the boat and crew. The Minnie was sixty feet long, ten feet wide, and was decked over. The crew consisted of thirty French-Canadian cordelliers, or towmen, a cook, a steersman and two bowmen, and a hunter with his horse. In a very small cabin aft there were two bunks. Forward there was a mast and sail for use when the wind was favorable—which was seldom. There was a big sweep oar on each side, and a number of poles were scattered along the deck to be used as occasion required. In the bow there was a four-pound howitzer, loaded with plenty of powder, and a couple of quarts of trade balls, in case of an attack by Indians, which was not at all improbable.

By the channel it was called eight hundred miles from Fort Union to Fort Benton, where we hoped to arrive in two months. After the first day's experience, I thought that we should be fortunate if we reached the place in two years. From morning until night the cordelliers toiled as I had never seen men toil before. It was a painful sight, those thirty men tugging on the long tow-rope as they floundered through water often waist-deep; through quicksand or mud so tenacious that the more unfortunate were dragged out of it gasping for breath and smeared with the stuff from head to foot. They frequently lost their footing on steep places and rolled down into deep water; banks of earth caved upon them; they were scratched and torn by rose-brush and bull-berry thorns; they were obliged to cut trails along the top of the banks in places, and to clear a way for the boat through dense masses of sawyers and driftwood.

A day or two after leaving Fort Union we narrowly escaped losing the boat, and the lives of all of us who were on it, in the treacherous swirling current. At the time the cordelliers were walking easily along a sandy shore under a high bank. Ahead of them, at the edge of the water, lay a dead buffalo bull, its rump partly eaten by the prowling animals. When the lead-man was within a few feet of it a big grizzly sprang toward him from the other side of the carcass, where it had lain asleep. The men dropped the rope and with loud cries sprang into the water, since they could not climb the bank. The boat at once turned broadside to the swift current, drifted against two sawyers, and began to turn turtle. The lower rail was already under water, and the horse had lost its footing and tumbled overboard, where it hung strangling, when by the greatest good fortune first one and then the other of the sawyers snapped under the strain, and the boat righted and swung in to the bank. We now had time to see what was going on above. The bear was just leaving the opposite shore and making for the timber; the men, dripping from their hasty bath, were gathered in a close group near the carcass, and were talking and gesticulating as only Frenchmen can. We suspected that something was wrong, and while the bowmen made the boat fast, the rest of us hurried up the shore. The group parted at our approach and disclosed one of their number — the lead-man on the rope — lying moaning on the sand. The bear had overtaken and mauled him terribly, and then, frightened probably by the loud cries of so many men, it took to the river and swam away. We got the wounded man aboard at once, and my uncle set his arm and made him as comfortable as possible. The hunter had saved his horse by cutting its rope and swimming with it to a landing far down stream. As soon as the tow-line was recovered we went on, thankful that the accident had been no worse.

Yet through it all they were cheerful and happy, and at the evening camp-fire my uncle was frequently obliged to speak harshly to keep them from shouting their voyageur songs, that might have brought some prowling war party of Indians down on us. The food of these men was meat—nothing but meat, washed down with a little tea. Sometimes they managed to dig a few *pommes blanches*, white, edible roots that were very palatable when roasted in the coals. Uncle Wesley and I had a box of hard crackers and a few pounds of flour and sugar. When they were gone, he told me, we should have no more until we sat down to our Christmas dinner. That did not worry me; I thought that if big, strong men could live on meat, a boy could, too.

The river wound like a snake through the great valley. There were long points only a mile or two across by land, but many times that distance round by the channel. Sometimes when we came to such a place Uncle Wesley and I would hunt across the bottom and then wait for the boat. On these trips I killed my first deer and elk and antelope—not to mention several more buffalo.

But Uncle Wesley was always uneasy when away from the boat; he was responsible for it and its cargo, which was worth more than a hundred thousand dollars in furs. Should anything happen to it while he was away from it, even for an hour's hunt, his hope of eventually becoming a member of the great company would have to be given up. Finally, after minute instructions in the proper handling of the rifle, I was allowed to accompany the hunter on his daily quests for meat.

Baptiste Rondin was a dreamy, gentle little Creole from Louisiana. He came from a good family, had not been taught to work, and had hated books, so he told me. So when misfortune came to his family, and he had to do something, he chose the position he now held in preference to others with more pay which the Chouteaus had offered him. When we started out in the morning, I would climb up behind him on the gentle old horse, and we would ride for miles up one side or the other of the river. We always saw various kinds of game soon after leaving the boat, but never attempted to kill any until some was found convenient to the shore of the river, where the boat could land and the meat easily be taken aboard.

Besides looking for game, we examined every dusty trail, every mudflat and sandbar, and constantly scanned the bottoms and the hills for signs of Indians. They were the great terror of the cordelliers; often a boat's crew was surprised and killed, or the cargo was destroyed.

We tied up one night four or five miles below the mouth of the Musselshell River, which my Uncle Wesley said Lewis and Clark had so named on account of the quantities of fossil shells that are found there.

Early the next morning Baptiste saddled the old horse, and we started out to hunt at the same time that the cordelliers hauled the rope tight and began their weary tramp.

We came to the lower edge of the big bottom at the mouth of the Musselshell. Opposite the mouth there was a heavily timbered island. One small band of antelope was the only game in sight between us and the Musselshell. On the other side of it, at the upper end of the bottom and close to the Missouri, there were a couple of hundred buffalo, some feeding, some lying down.

They were so far away that we rode boldly through the tall sage-brush to the little river, and across it to the outer edge of the strip of timber. There Baptiste told me to remain with the horse while he crept out to the herd and made a killing. I did not like being left alone. There were many fresh grizzly tracks on the river sands just behind me, and I was afraid of the terrible animals, so afraid that I did not dare to dismount and gather some strawberries which showed in the grass at the horse's feet.

The passing minutes seemed hours. The tall sage-brush out ahead had swallowed Baptiste. By rising in the stirrups I could just see the backs of some of the distant buffalo. A sudden splash in the river made my heart flutter, and I quickly turned to see what had caused it.

Here and there between the trees and brush its glistening surface was in plain view, and through one opening I saw something more terrible than a whole band of grizzlies: an Indian crossing toward me. I saw his face, painted red with blue bars across the cheeks;

I noted that he wore leather clothing; that a shield hung suspended from his left arm; that in his right hand he grasped a bow and a few arrows.

All this I noted in an instant of time; and then nearer to me, and more to the right, a stick snapped, and I turned my head to see another Indian in the act of letting an arrow fly at me. I yelled and gave the horse such a thump with the stock of my rifle that he made a long, quick leap. That was a lucky thing for me. The arrow aimed at my body cut through my coat sleeve and gashed my left arm just above the elbow.

I yelled frantically for Baptiste and urged the horse on through the sage-brush. I looked back, and saw that Indians all up and down the stream were leaving the timber and running toward me. I looked ahead and saw the smoke of Baptiste's gun, heard the report, saw the buffalo bunch up and then scurry westward for the nearest hills.

The thought came to me that I could pick

the hunter up, and that the old horse would easily carry us beyond the possibility of an attack by Indians afoot. That hope was shattered a moment later. The buffalo suddenly circled and came back into the bottom, and I saw that they had been turned by some Indians at the edge of the hills. Indians were strung out clear across the flat, were leaping through the sage-brush toward us, and shouting their dreadful war-cry; they were hemming us in on the south, and the great river cut off our retreat to the north.

I urged the old horse on, determined to reach Baptiste and die by his side, but the Indians who had appeared on the hills were now quite near him. I saw him raise his rifle and fire at the one in the lead, then turn and run a few steps and spring from the high cut-bank into the river. But just before jumping he paused, and raising a hand, motioned to me to turn back.

To turn back! Accustomed to obeying him, I sawed on the bridle and the horse stopped. I looked over my shoulder, and saw that the nearest of the Indians were not three hundred yards from me. In my distress I cried, "What shall I do? Oh, what shall I — what can I do to escape?"

CHAPTER II

I DO not know why I cried out. Of course there was no one to answer, to advise, or assist me. I have often noticed that in times of stress men shout the questions that they ask themselves. Why had Baptiste motioned me to go back, when by doing so I must run right into the Indians? I must have misunderstood his signal. Clearly, my only chance of escape was the same as his, and that was by the river.

Pummeling the old horse with rifle-stock and heels, I headed him for the stream. Not straight toward it, where the bank was apparently very high, but obliquely, toward a point not far above the mouth of the Musselshell. There the bank was certainly not high, for the tips of water-willows peeped above it.

In a few moments I was close enough to look over it. Between the narrow strip of willows and the edge of the water there was an oozy mudflat, fifty yards wide, impassable for man or horse.

I looked back at the enemy, and saw that when I had turned downstream, those toward the upper end of the bottom had given up the chase, while the rest had turned with me and run faster than ever. Thus there was a wide gap between the two parties, and I circled toward it, as my last chance. First up the river for several hundred yards, then straight south, away from it. Both parties immediately perceived my intention, and spurted to close the gap. Harder and harder I thumped the horse, although by this time he had waked up, and was entering into the spirit of the flight. The distance between the two parties of Indians was now not more than three hundred yards, and I was more than that from the point for which we all were heading; but to offset this I was covering the ground much faster than they were.

The Indians were now yelling frightfully, to encourage one another to greater speed. I could see their painted faces, and a little later their fierce eyes.

The gap was very small now; they began shooting, and several pieces of lead ripped by me with the sound of tearing paper. I did not try to use my rifle. In that first experience there was no anger in my heart against the enemy, nothing but fear of them.

I felt, rather than saw, that they would be unable to head me off, if only by a narrow margin, and I bent low over the horse to make myself as small a target as possible. More guns boomed close on each side of me. Arrows whizzed, too, and the shaft of one struck my rifle-stock, glanced from it, and cut the skin on the back of my hand. That was when I passed right between the two parties.

In a dazed way, I kept urging the horse on, until presently it dawned on me that I was past the danger point. Having looked back to make sure of this, I changed my course, crossed the Musselshell, and went on down the bottom, and then along the shore of the river several miles, until I came to the boat.

When the cordelliers saw me returning in such haste, they knew that something was wrong. They ceased towing, and let the boat drift in to the bank, in such a position that I rode right on the deck. I was still so frightened that it was difficult for me to talk, but my uncle, guessing the parts of the story which I omitted, ordered all the men aboard. In a few minutes we were at the other shore of the river.

The cordelliers objected to going on with the tow-line, but my uncle was firm that they should start without delay, and they did. The steersman, an old and tried employee, was sent ahead of them to scout, and Uncle Wesley took his place at the sweep. The howitzer was freshly primed, and one of the men instructed to stand by, ready to aim and fire it. I was anxious about Baptiste, and although my uncle told me not to worry, I doubted if we should ever see him again.

In a couple of hours we arrived off the island opposite the mouth of the Musselshell, and lo! Baptiste came out of the brush at the lower end of it, and signaled us to take him aboard. That was done with the skiff. As soon as he came on deck he ran to me, in his impetuous French way, gave me a hug and a thump on the back, and exclaimed, "It is my brave boy! And he is safe! One little wound in the hand? That is nothing. Now, tell me how you made the escape."

But at this moment my uncle came to consult the hunter, and my story was deferred. I learned from Baptiste later that the Indians were Crees, probably on their way south, to raid the Crow horse herds.

By this time we had passed the island. Baptiste was just asking us to note how high the cut-bank was from which he had jumped into the stream, when the whole party of Indians rose out of the sage-brush at the edge of it, and with much yelling, fired their guns at us. As the distance was three or four hundred yards, only a few of their balls struck anywhere near the boat. Uncle Wesley himself sprang to the howitzer, swung it round, tilted up the barrel, and fired it. Some of the balls dropped into the water near the far shore, several spatted little puffs of dust out of the dry cut-bank, and others must have passed right among the war party. Anyway, the Indians all ducked down and ran back from the bluff. We saw no more of them.

Ever since leaving the mouth of the Yellowstone we had been passing through the extraordinary formation of the Bad Lands. From this point onward the scenery became more and more wonderful. Boy that I was, I was so deeply impressed with the strange grandeur of it all that the sensations I experienced were at times actually oppressive. At every turn there was something to astonish the eye. There were gleaming white and gray turreted castles, perched high above the stream; cities of clustering domes and towers and minarets, all wrought by the elements from sandstones of varying hardness, but all so apparently real as to suggest that men and women in mediæval dress might pass out of the gates in the walls at any moment.

We arrived at Fort Benton just ninety days after leaving Fort Union. The flag was raised and cannon fired in our honor, and more than five thousand Blackfeet, headed by the factor, Alexander Culbertson, and the employees of the fort, crowded to the river-bank to give us welcome.

I was astonished to see so many Indians. I noticed that they were tall, fine-looking men and women; that they wore beautiful garments of tanned skins; that their hair was done up in long, neat braids; that many of the leading men shook hands with my uncle, and seemed glad to meet him.

My uncle introduced me to that great man, the factor, who patted me kindly on the shoulder. With him we went into the fort, where, just as we passed through the big gate, a tall, handsome Indian woman, wearing a neat calico dress, a plaid shawl, and beautifully embroidered moccasins, came running to us, threw her arms round my uncle, and kissed him. I must have looked as surprised as I felt, especially when I noted that he was very glad to meet her. Having spoken a few words to her, which I could n't understand, he turned to me. "Thomas," he said, "this is your aunt. I hope that you and she will become great friends."

I was now more surprised than ever, but tried not to show it as I answered, "Yes, sir."

At that the woman gave a smile that was pleasant to see, and the next instant she had me in her arms and was kissing me, smoothing my hair, and talking Blackfoot to me in her strangely clear and pleasant voice. My uncle interpreted. "She says that she wants to be your mother now; that she wants you to love her, to come to her for everything you need."

I do not know just what it was, — her voice, her appearance, the motherly feeling of her arms round me, — but there was something about this Indian woman that made my heart go straight out to her. I gave her hand a squeeze, while tears came to my eyes as I snuggled up close to her. Right willingly I went with her and Uncle Wesley to the room in the far end of the long adobe building forming the east side of the fort, which he said was to be our home for a long time to come.

It was the kind of room that gave one a restful feeling at sight. Opposite the doorway was a big fireplace of stone and adobe, with hooks above the mantel for rifles and powder-horns and ball-pouches. Two windows on the courtyard side afforded plenty of light. There were a strong table and comfortable chairs, all home-made. A settee covered with buffalo-robes was placed before the fire. A curtained set of shelves in the corner contained the dishes and cooking-utensils. The north end of the room was partitioned off for a sleeping-place. My bed,

I was told, would be the buffalo-robe couch under the window at the right of the door.

The next day my uncle took me all round the fort and made me known to the different employees — clerks and tailors, carpenters and blacksmiths, and the men of the trade-room. The fort was a large one, about three hundred feet square, all of adobe. Entering the front gate, you saw that three long buildings, of which the easterly one was two stories high, formed three sides of the quadrangle, and that a high wall containing the gate formed the fourth, or south side, facing the river. The outer walls of the buildings were thus the defensive walls of the fort. They were protected against assault by two-storied bastions, with cannon at the southeast and northwest corners. All the tribes of the Northwest together could not have taken the place by assault without the loss of thousands of their force, and they knew it.

Before night the keel-boat was unloaded, and our trunks were brought in and unpacked. My mother's little library and my school-books filled a new set of shelves, and that evening I began, under my uncle's direction, a course of study and reading, preparatory to going East to school in the following year.

No boy ever had a happier time than I had in that fort so far beyond the borders of civilization. Day in and day out there was always something worth while going on. Hundreds, and often thousands, of Indians came in to trade, and I found endless pleasure in mingling with them and learned their language and customs. In this I was encouraged by Tsistsaki (Little Bird Woman), my uncle's wife. She had no children, and all her natural mother love was given to me. In her way of thinking, nothing that I did could be wrong, and the best of everything was not good enough for me. The beautifully embroidered buckskin suits and moccasins she made for me fairly dazzled the eye with their blaze of color. These were not for everyday wear, but I took every possible occasion for putting them on, and strutted around, the envy of all the Indian boys in the country.

The winter passed all too quickly. With the approach of spring my uncle began to plan for my long trip to St. Louis, and thence to the home of my mother's Connecticut friend, where I was to prepare for Princeton. I said nothing to him, but I had many talks with my aunt-mother, Tsistsaki; and one night we poured out such a torrent of reasons why I should not go, ending our pleadings with tears, that he gave in to us, and agreed that I should grow up in the fur trade.

A frequent visitor in our cozy room in the fort was a nephew of Tsistsaki, a boy several years older than I. We liked each other at sight, and every time we met we became firmer friends than ever. "Friend" means much more to Indians — at least, to the Blackfeet — than it does to white people. Once friends, Indians are always friends. They almost never quarrel. So it came to be with Pitamakan (Eagle Running) and myself.

My uncle Wesley was as much pleased as his wife. One day he said to me, "Pitamakan is an honest, good-hearted boy, and brave, too. He gets all that from his father, who is one of the very best and most trustworthy Indians in all this country, and from his mother, who is a woman of fine character. See to it that you keep his friendship."

Except, of course, Baptiste Rondin, the hunter of the fort, Pitamakan was almost the only one with whom I was allowed to go after the buffalo and the other game which swarmed on the plains near by. What with my daily studies, occasional hunts, and the constant pleasure I had in the life of the fort, time fairly flew; no day was too long. And yet, for four years, I never once went more than five miles from the fort.

During this time my one great desire was to go on a trip into the Rocky Mountains. Clearly visible from the high plains to the north and south of the river, their pine-clad slopes and sharp, bare peaks always seemed to draw me to explore their almost unknown fastnesses.

In the fall of 1860 there came an opportunity for me to do this. The Small Robes band of the Blackfeet, of which Pitamakan's father, White Wolf (Mah-kwi'-yi ksik-si-num), was chief, outfitted at the fort for an expedition to trap beaver along the foot of the great mountains, and, much to my surprise and delight, I was permitted to accompany them.

At this time there were ninety lodges—about six hundred people—of the Small Robes (I-nuk-siks) band of the Blackfeet. They had several thousand horses, and when the moving camp was strung out on the plain, the picturesque riders, the pack-animals laden with queerly shaped, painted rawhide and leather pouches and sacks, made a pageant of moving color that was very impressive.

Our first camp after leaving the fort was

on the Teton River. A couch was made up for me in White Wolf's lodge. The lodge of the plains Indians was the most comfortable portable shelter ever devised by man. One of average size was made of sixteen large cow buffalo-hides, tanned into soft leather, cut to shape, and sewed together with sinew thread.

This cone-shaped "lodge skin" was stretched over tough, slender poles of mountain-pine, and the lower edge, or skirt, was pegged so that it was at least four inches above the ground. Within, a leather lining, firmly weighted to the ground by the couches and household impedimenta of the occupants, extended upward for five or six feet, where it was tied to a rope that was fastened to the poles clear round. There was a space as wide as the thickness of the poles between the "skin" and the lining, so that the cold, outside air rushing up through it created a draft for the fire, and carried the smoke out of the open space at the top. This lining, of course, prevented the cold air from coming into the lower part of the lodge, so that even in the coldest weather a small fire was enough for comfort.

Traveling leisurely up the Teton River, we came in three or four days to the foot of the great range. There we went into camp for several weeks, long enough for the hunters to trap most of the beavers, not only on the main stream, but on all its little tributaries. Pitamakan and I had twelve traps, and were partners in the pursuit of the animals.

From the Teton we moved northward to Back-Fat Creek, now Dupuyer Creek. From there we went to the Two Medicine waters, and then on to the Cut-Bank River. The trapping area of this stream was small. On the first day of our camp there Pitamakan and I foolishly went hunting, with the result that when, on the next day, we began looking for a place to set our traps, we found that all the beaver-ponds and bank-workings had been occupied by the other trappers.

It was late in the afternoon, after we had

followed up the south fork to a tremendous walled cañon, where it was impossible for the beavers to make dams and homes, that we made this discovery. Our disappointment was keen, for from Cut-Bank the camp was to return to Fort Benton, and we had only thirty-seven of the fifty beaver pelts that we had planned to take home with us.

We were sitting on a well-worn trail that stretched along the mountainside above the cañon, when Pitamakan suddenly exclaimed: —

"Listen to me! We will get the rest of the beaver! You see this trail? Well, it crosses this backbone of the world, and is made by the other-side people, — the Kootenays and the Flatheads, — so that they can come over to our plains and steal our buffalo. You can see that it has not been used this summer. It will not be used at all now, since winter is so near. Now, down on the other side there are many streams in the great forest, and no doubt there are beavers in them. We will go over there to-morrow, and in a few days' trapping we will catch enough to make up the number we set out to get."

This plan seemed good to me, and I said so at once. We left the traps on the trail and started to camp, to prepare for an early start in the morning. We decided to say nothing to any one of our intentions, to White Wolf least of all, lest he should forbid our going.

At dusk we picketed near camp two horses that we selected for the trip, and during the evening we refilled our powder-horns and ball-pouches to the neck. Rising the next morning before any of the others were awake, and each taking a heavy buffalo-robe from our bedding, we quietly left the lodge, saddled and mounted our horses, and rode away. Some dried meat and buffalo back fat taken from the lodge furnished us a substantial breakfast.

The trail was plain and easy to follow.

We picked up the traps, and mounting steadily, arrived at the extreme summit of the great range not long after midday. From where we stood, the trail ran slightly downward, along a narrow divide, across to the next mountain. The south side of the divide was a sheer drop of several thousand feet. The top was a narrow, jagged knife of rock, along which a man could not have passed on foot. On the north side the sharp reef dropped almost precipitously to a narrow and exceedingly steep slope of fine shale rock, which terminated at the edge of a precipice of fearful depth.

It was along this shale slope that the trail ran, but there were no signs of it now, for the tracks of the last horses that passed had been filled. Even while we stood there, small particles of shale were constantly rolling and tinkling down it and off into abysmal space. Shuddering, I proposed that we turn back, but Pitamakan made light of the danger.

"I have been here before, and know what to do," he said. "I can make it so that we can safely cross it."

With a long, thin and narrow slab of rock he began gouging a trail out of the steep slide. The small and the large pieces of detritus which he dislodged rattled off the edge of the cliff, but strain my ears as I might, I could not hear them strike bottom. It was fully a hundred yards across this dangerous place, but Pitamakan soon made his way along it, and back to me.

His path seemed more fit for coyotes than for horses, but he insisted that it was wide enough, and started leading his animal out on it. There was nothing for me to do but to follow with mine. When part way across, my horse's hind feet broke down the little path, and he went with the sliding shale for several feet, all the time madly pawing to get back on the sound portion on which I stood. When I tried to help him by pulling on the lead-rope, the shale began sliding under my feet. At that, Pitamakan, starting to run with his horse, shouted to me to do the same.

For the rest of the way across, the strain on me and my animal was killing. We tore out all trace of the path in our efforts to keep from going down and off the slide. Wherever we put down our feet the shale started slipping, and the struggle to climb faster than it slipped exhausted our strength. When finally we did reach the firm rock where my companion stood waiting, we were utterly fatigued and dripping with sweat.

Pitamakan's face was ashy gray from the strain of watching my struggles. He drew me to him, and I could feel him trembling, while he said, in a choking voice, "Oh, I thought you would never get here, and I just had to stand and look, unable to help you in any way! I did n't know. I should have made a wider, firmer path."

We sat down, and he told me about this pass: that after the winter snows came neither man nor horse could cross it, since the least movement would start the snow sliding. Three Blackfeet had once lost their lives there. In that manner, the avalanche which they loosened had swept them with it over the cliff, to the horror of their comrades who stood looking on. Upon our return, he said, he would make a safe path there, if it took him all day to finish the task.

Soon we went on, turned the shoulder of the twin mountain, and felt that we had come into another world. Near by there were some tremendous peaks, some of them covered with great fields of ice, which I learned later were true glaciers.

In other ways, too, this west side was different from the east side of the Rockies. As far as we could see there were no plains, only one great, dark, evergreen forest that covered the slopes of the mountains and filled the endless valleys. Here, too, the air was different; it was damp and heavy, and odorous of plants that grow in moist climates.

Working our way from ledge to ledge down the mountain, we came, toward sunset, to what my friend called the Salt Springs. Farther west than this point he had never been.

Early the next morning we pushed on, for we were anxious to reach the low valleys where the beavers were to be found.

Still following the trail, we struck, about mid-afternoon, a large stream bordered with alder, cottonwood, and willow, the bark of which is the beaver's favorite food. There were some signs of the animals here, but as we expected to find them more plentiful farther down, we kept on until nearly sundown, when we came to a fine grass meadow bordering the now larger river. Here was feed for the horses; in a pond at the upper end of the meadow there were five beaver lodges.

"Here is the place for us," said Pitamakan. "Let us hurry and picket the horses, and kill a deer; night is at hand."

We started to ride into the timber to unsaddle, when we heard a heavy trampling and crackling of sticks off to the left of the beaver-pond, and so sat still, rifles ready, expecting to see a band of elk come into the open.

A moment later thirty or forty Indians, men, women, and children, rode into the meadow. Perceiving us, the men whipped up their horses and came racing our way.

"They are Kootenays! It is useless to fire at them, or to run!" Pitamakan exclaimed. "I do not think they will harm us. Anyhow, look brave; pretend that you are not afraid."

The men who surrounded us were tall and powerfully built. For what seemed to me an endless time, they sat silently staring, and noting every detail of our outfit. There was something ominous in their behavior; there came to me an almost uncontrollable impulse to make a move of some kind. It was their leader who broke the suspense.

"*In-is-saht!*" (Dismount!) he commanded, in Blackfoot, and we reluctantly obeyed.

At that they all got off their horses, and then at word from the chief, each crowding and pushing to be first, they stripped us of everything we had. One man got my rifle; another the ammunition; another snatched off my belt, with its knife, and the little pouch containing flint, steel, and punk, while the chief and another, who seemed to be a great warrior, seized the ropes of our horses. And there we were, stripped of everything that we possessed except the clothes we stood in.

At that the chief broke out laughing, and so did the rest. Finally, commanding silence, he said to us, in very poor Blackfoot:—

"As you are only boys, we will not kill you. Return to your chief, and tell him that we keep our beaver for ourselves, just as the plains people keep the buffalo for themselves. Now go."

There was nothing to do but obey him,

and we started. One man followed us a few steps, and struck Pitamakan several blows across the back with his whip. At that my friend broke out crying; not because of the pain, but because of the terrible humiliation. To be struck by any one was the greatest of all insults; and my friend was powerless to resent it.

Looking back, we saw the Kootenays move on through the meadow and disappear in the timber. Completely dazed by our great misfortune, we mechanically took our back trail, and seldom speaking, walked on and on. When night came, rain began to fall and the wind rose to a gale in the tree-tops. At that Pitamakan shook his head, and said, dejectedly, "At this season rain down here means snow up on top. We must make strong medicine if we are ever to see our people again."

Hungry and without food or weapons for killing any game, wet and without shelter or any means of building a fire, we certainly were in a terrible plight. Worse still, if it was snowing on the summit, if winter had really set in, we must inevitably perish. I remembered hearing the old trappers say that winter often began in October in the Rocky Mountains; and this day was well on in November! "Pitamakan! We are not going to survive this!" I cried.

For answer, he began singing the coyote song, the Blackfoot hunter's prayer for good luck. It sounded weird and melancholy enough there in the darkening forest.

CHAPTER III

"THERE! Something tells me that will bring us good luck," said Pitamakan, when he had finished the medicine song. "First of all, we must find shelter from the rain. Let us hurry and search for it up there along the foot of the cliffs."

Leaving the trail, we pushed our way up the steep slope of the valley, through underbrush that dropped a shower of water on us at the slightest touch. There were only a few hundred yards between us and the foot of the big wall which shot high above the tops of the pines, but by the time we arrived there night had fairly come. At this point a huge pile of boulders formed the upper edge of the slope, and for a moment we stood undecided which way to turn. "Toward home, of course!" Pitamakan exclaimed, and led the way along the edge of the boulders, and finally to the cliff. There in fron of us was a small, jagged aperture, and stoop ing down, we tried to see what it was like inside.. The darkness, however, was impen etrable.

I could hear my companion sniffing; soom he asked, "Do you smell anything?"

But I could detect no odor other than that of the dank forest floor, and said so.

"Well, I think that I smell bear!" he whispered, and we both leaped back, and then stealthily drew away from the place But the rain was falling now in a heavy downpour; the rising wind lashed it in our faces and made the forest writhe and creak and snap. Every few moments some old dead pine went down with a crash. It was a terrible night.

"We can't go on!" said Pitamakan. "Perhaps I was mistaken. Bears do not lie down for their winter sleep until the snow has covered up their food. We must go back and take our chance of one being there in that hole."

We felt our way along the foot of the cliff until we came to the place. There we knelt down, hand in hand, sniffed once more, and exclaimed, "*Kyaiyo!*" (Bear!)

"But not strong; only a little odor, as if one had been here last winter," Pitamakan added. "The scent of one sticks in a place a long time."

Although I was shivering so much from the cold and wet that my teeth rattled, I managed to say, "Come on! We've got to go in there."

Crawling inch by inch, feeling of the ground ahead, and often stopping to sniff the air and listen, we made our cautious way inside, and presently came to a fluffy heap of dried grass, small twigs and leaves that rustled at our touch.

"Ah, we survive, brother!" Pitamakan exclaimed, in a cheerful voice. "The bear has been here and made himself a bed for the winter; they always do that in the month of falling leaves. He is n't here now, though, and if he does come we will yell loud and scare him away."

Feeling round now to learn the size of the place, we found that it was small and low, and sloped to the height of a couple of feet at the back. Having finished the examination, we burrowed down into the grass and leaves, snuggled close together, and covered ourselves as well as we could. Little by little we stopped shivering, and after a while felt comfortably warm, although wet.

We fell to talking then of our misfortune, and planning various ways to get out of the bad fix we were in. Pitamakan was all for following the Kootenays, stealing into their camp at night, and trying to recover not only our horses, but, if possible, our rifles also. I made the objection that even if we got a whole night's start of the Kootenays, they, knowing the trails better than we did, would overtake us before we could ride to the summit. We finally agreed to follow the trail of our enemies and have a look at their camp;

we might find some way of getting back what they had taken.

We really slept well. In the morning I awoke first, and looking out, saw nothing but thick, falling snow. I nudged my companion, and together we crept to the mouth of the cave. The snow was more than a foot deep in front of us, and falling so fast that only the nearest of the big pines below could be seen. The weather was not cold, certainly not much below freezing, but it caused our damp clothing to feel like ice against the skin. We crept back into our nest, shivering again.

"With this snow on the ground, it would be useless to try to take anything from the Kootenays," I said.

"True enough. They could follow our tracks and easily overtake us," Pitamakan agreed.

As he said no more for a long time, and would not even answer when I asked a question, I, too, became silent. But not for long;

so many fears and doubts were oppressing me that I had to speak. "We had better start on, then, and try to cross the summit."

Pitamakan shook his head slowly. "Neither we nor any one else will cross the summit until summer comes again. This is winter. See, the snow is almost to our knees out there; up on top it is over our heads."

"Then we must die right here!" I exclaimed.

For answer, my partner began the coyote prayer song, and kept singing it over and over, except when he would break out into prayers to the sun, and to Old Man — the World-Maker — to give us help. There in the low little cave his song sounded muffled and hollow enough. Had I not been watching his face, I must have soon begged him to stop, it was so mournful and depressing.

But his face kept brightening and brightening until he actually smiled; and finally he turned to me and said, "Do not worry, brother. Take courage. They have put new thoughts into me."

I asked what the thoughts were, and he replied by asking what we most needed.

"Food, of course," I said. "I am weak from hunger."

"I thought you would say that!" he exclaimed. "It is always food with white people. Get up in the morning and eat a big meal; at midday, another; at sunset, another. If even one of these is missed, they say they are starving. No, brother, we do not most need food. We could go without it half a moon and more, and the long fast would only do us good."

I did not believe that. It was the common belief in those times that a person could live for only a few days without food.

"No, it is not food; it is fire that we most need," Pitamakan continued. "Were we to go out in that snow and get wet and then have no means of drying and warming ourselves, we should die."

"Well, then, we must just lie here and wait for the snow to melt away," I said, "for without flint and steel we can have no fire."

"Then we will lie here until next summer. This country is different from ours of the plains. There the snow comes and goes many times during the winter; here it only gets deeper and deeper, until the sun beats Cold-Maker, and comes north again."

I believed that to be true, for I remembered that my uncle had told me once that there were no chinook winds on the west side of the range. So I proposed what had been on my mind for some time: that we go to the camp of the Kootenays and beg them to give us shelter.

"If they didn't kill us, they would only beat us and drive us away. No, we cannot go to them," said Pitamakan decidedly. "Now don't look so sad; we shall have fire."

He must have read my thoughts, for he added, "I see that you don't believe that I can make fire. Listen! Before you white people came with your flints and steels, we had it. Old Man himself taught us how to make it. I have never seen it made in the old way because my people got the new way before I was born. But I have often heard the older ones tell how it used to be made, and I believe that I can do it myself. It is easy. You take a small, dry, hard stick like an arrow-shaft, and twirl it between the palms of your hands, or with a bowstring, while the point rests in a hole in a piece of dry wood, with fine shreds of birch bark in it. The twirling stick heats these and sets them on fire."

Although I did not understand this explanation very well, I yet had some faith that Pitamakan could make the fire. He added that he would not try it until the weather cleared, and we could go round in the timber without getting wet except from the knees down.

We lay there in the bear's bed all that day. At sunset the snow ceased falling, but when the clouds disappeared, the weather turned much colder, and it was well for us that the heat of our bodies had pretty thoroughly dried our clothing. As it was, we shivered all through the night, and were very miserable.

Out in the darkness we heard some animal scraping through the snow, and feared that it might be the bear come to get into its bed. We had talked about that. If it was a black bear, we were safe enough, because they are the most cowardly of all animals, and even when wounded, will not attack a man. But what if it were a big grizzly! We both knew tales enough of their ferocity. Only that summer a woman, picking berries, had been killed by one.

So when we heard those soft footsteps we yelled; stopped and listened, and yelled again, and again, until we were hoarse. Then we listened. All was still. Whatever had roused us was gone, but fear that a grizzly would come shuffling in kept us awake.

Day came long before the sun rose above

the tremendous peaks that separated us from the plains. Much as we ached to crawl out of the cave and run and jump, we lay still until the sun had warmed the air a bit. The night before I had been ravenously hungry; but now my hunger had largely passed, and Pitamakan said that I would soon forget all about food.

"But we can't live all winter without eating!" I objected.

"Of course not," he replied. "As soon as we have fire, we will go hunting and kill game. Then we will make us a comfortable lodge. Oh, we're going to be very comfortable here before many days pass."

"But the Kootenays!" I objected. "They will come again and drive us on, or kill us!"

"Just now they are moving out of the mountains as fast as they can go, and will not return until summer comes again."

When we finally crawled out after our long rest, we saw that a bear really had been near us in the night. It had come walking along the slope, close to the foot of the cliff, until right in front of the cave, and then, startled, no doubt, by our yells, had gone leaping straight down into the timber. The short impressions of its claws in the snow proved it to have been a black bear. We were glad of that; another night, fear, at least, would not prevent us from sleeping.

Both of us were clothed for summer hunting, I in buckskin trousers and flannel shirt, with no underclothing or socks. Pitamakan wore buffalo cow-leather leggings, breech-clout, and, fortunately, a shirt like mine that his aunt had given him. Neither of us had coat or waistcoat, but in place of them, capotes, hooded coats reaching to our knees, made of white blanket by the tailor at the fort. The snow looked very cold to step into with only thin buckskin moccasins on our feet, and I said so.

"We will remedy that," said Pitamakan. He pulled off his capote, tore a couple of strips from the skirt of it, and then did the same with mine. With these we wrapped our feet, pulled our moccasins on over them, and felt that our toes were frost-proof.

The snow was knee-deep. Stepping into it bravely, we made our way down the slope and into the timber. There it was not so deep, for a part of the fall had lodged in the thick branches of the pines. We came upon the tracks of deer and elk, and presently saw a fine white-tail buck staring curiously at us. The sight of his rounded, fat body brought the hungry feeling back to me, and I expressed it with a plaintive "*Hai-yah!*" of longing.

Pitamakan understood. "Never mind," he said, as the animal broke away, waving its broad flag as if in derision. "Never mind. We will be eating fat ribs to-morrow, perhaps; surely on the next day."

That talk seemed so big to me that I said nothing, asked no question, as we went on down the hill. Before reaching the river we saw several more deer, a lone bull moose and a number of elk; the valley was full of game, driven from the high mountains by the storm.

The river was not frozen, nor was there any snow on the low, wet, rocky bars to hinder our search for a knife. That was what we were to look for, just as both Pitamakan's and my own ancestors had searched, in prehistoric times, for sharp-edged tools in glacial drift and river wash. I was to look for flint and "looks-like-ice rock," as the Blackfeet call obsidian. As I had never seen any obsidian, except in the form of very small, shiny arrow-points, it was not strange that Pitamakan found a nodule of it on a bar that I had carefully gone over. It was somewhat the shape of a football, rusty black, and coated with splotches of stuff that looked like whitewash. I could not believe that it was what we sought until he cracked it open and I saw the glittering fragments.

Pitamakan had never seen any flint or

obsidian flaked and chipped into arrow-points and knives, but he had often heard the old people tell how it was done, and now he tried to profit by the information. With a small stone for a hammer, he gently tapped one of the fragments, and succeeded in splintering it into several thin, sharp-edged flakes. Carefully taking up all the fragments and putting them at the foot of a tree for future use, we went in search of material for the rest of the fire-making implements.

We knew from the start that finding them would not be easy, for before the snow came, rain had thoroughly soaked the forest, and what we needed was bone-dry wood. We had hunted for an hour or more, when a half-dozen ruffed grouse flushed from under the top of a fallen tree and flew up into the branches of a big fir, where they sat and craned their necks. Back came my hungry feeling; here was a chance to allay it. "Come on, let's get some stones and try to kill those birds!" I cried.

Away we went to the shore of the river, gathered a lot of stones in the skirts of our capotes, and hurried back to the tree. The birds were still there, and we began throwing at the one lowest down. We watched the course of each whizzing stone with intense eagerness, groaning, "*Ai-ya!*" when it went wide of the mark. Unlike white boys, Indian youths are very inexpert at throwing stones, for the reason that they constantly carry a better weapon, the bow, and begin at a very early age to hunt small game with it. I could cast the stones much more accurately than Pitamakan, and soon he handed what he had left to me.

Although I made some near shots, and sent the stones clattering against the branches and zipping through the twigs, the bird never once moved, except to flutter a wing when a missile actually grazed it or struck the limb close to its feet. With the last stone of the lot I hit a grouse, and as it started fluttering down we made a rush for the foot of the tree, whooping wildly over our success, and frightening the rest of the covey so that they flew away.

The wounded bird lodged for a moment in a lower branch, toppled out of that into another, fluttered from that down into clear space. Pitamakan sprang to catch it, and grasped only the air; for the bird righted itself, sailed away and alighted in the snow, fifty yards distant. We ran after it as fast as we could. It was hurt. We could see that it had difficulty in holding up its head, and that its mouth was open. We felt certain of our meat. But no! Up it got when we were about to make our pounce, and half fluttered and half sailed another fifty yards or so. Again and again it rose, we hot after it, and finally it crossed the river. But that did not daunt us. The stream was wide there, running in a still sweep over a long bar; and we crossed, and in our hurry, splashed ourselves until we were wet above the waist. Then, after all, the grouse rose long before we came anywhere near it, and this time flew on and on until lost to sight!

Our disappointment was too keen to be put into words. Dripping wet and as miserable a pair of boys as ever were, we stood there in the cold snow and looked sadly at each other. "Oh, well, come on," said Pitamakan. "What is done is done. We will now get the wood we want and make a fire to dry ourselves."

He led off, walked to a half-fallen fir, and from the under side broke off just what we were looking for — a hard, dry spike about twice the diameter of a lead-pencil and a foot or more in length. That did seem to be good luck, and our spirits rose. We went out to the shore of the river, where I was set to rounding off the base of the spike and sharpening the point, first by rubbing it on a coarse-grained rock, and then smoothing it with a flake of obsidian. I ruined the edge of the first piece by handling it too vigorously; the brittle stone had to be forced slowly and diagonally along the place to be cut.

Pitamakan, meanwhile, was hunting a suitable piece of wood for the drill to work in. Hard wood, he had heard the old people say, was necessary for this, and here the only growth of the kind was birch.

By the time I got the drill shaped, he had found none that was dry, and I was glad to help in the search, for I was nearly frozen from standing still so long in my wet clothes. Up and down the river we went, and back into the forest, examining every birch that appeared to be dead. Every one that we found was rotten, or only half dry. It was by the merest chance that we found the very thing: a beaver-cutting of birch, cast by the spring freshet under a projecting ledge of rock, where it was protected from the rains. It was almost a foot in diameter and several feet long. We rubbed a coarse stone against the centre of it until the place was flat and a couple of inches wide, and in that started a small hole with the obsidian. This was slow work, for the glasslike substance constantly broke under the pressure needed to make it cut into the wood. It was late in the day when the gouging was finished, and we prepared to put our tools to the test.

This was an occasion for prayer. Pitamakan so earnestly entreated his gods to pity us, to make our work successful, and thus save our lives, that, unsympathetic as I was with his beliefs, I could not help being moved. I wanted to be stoical; to keep up a brave appearance to the last; but this pathetic prayer to heathen gods, coming as it did when I was weak from hunger and exposure, was too much. To this day I remember the exact words of it, too long to repeat here. I can translate only the closing sentence: "Also, have pity on us because of our dear people on the other side of the range, who are even now weeping in their lodges because we do not return to them."

When he had finished the prayer, Pitamakan took the drill in the palms of his hands and set the point of it in the small, rough hole in the birch. We had already gathered some dry birch bark, and I held some of it, shredded into a fluffy mass, close round the drill and the pole.

"Now, fire come!" Pitamakan exclaimed, and began to twirl the drill between his hands, at the same time pressing it firmly down in the hole.

But no smoke came. What was the reason? He stopped and raised the drill; we felt of it and the hole; both were very hot, and I suggested that we take turns drilling, changing about in the least possible time. We tried it, and oh, how anxiously we watched for success, drilling and drilling for our very lives, drilling turn about until our muscles were so strained that we could not give the stick another twirl! Then we dropped back and stared at each other. Our experiment had failed. Night was coming on.

Our wet clothing was beginning to freeze, and there was the river between us and the shelter of our cave.

The outlook seemed hopeless, and I said so. Pitamakan said nothing; his eyes had a strange, vacant expression. "We can do nothing," I repeated. "Right here we have to die."

Still he did not answer, or even look at me, and I said to myself, "He has gone mad!"

CHAPTER IV

IF they will not do," Pitamakan muttered, rising stiffly, while the ice on his leggings crackled, "why, I'll cut off a braid of my hair."

I was now sure that our troubles had weakened his mind; no Indian in his right senses would think of cutting off his hair.

"Pitamakan! What is the trouble with you?" I asked, looking up anxiously at him.

"Why, nothing is the matter," he replied. "Nothing is the matter. We must now try to work the drill with a bow. If our moccasin strings are too rotten to bear the strain, I'll have to make a bow cord by cutting off some of my hair and braiding it."

It was a great relief to know that he was sane enough, but I had little faith in this new plan, and followed listlessly as he went here and there, testing the branches of willow and birch. Finally, he got from the river shore one stone that was large and smooth, and another that had a sharp edge. Then, scraping the snow away from the base of a birch shoot a couple of inches in diameter, he laid the smooth stone at its base. Next he bade me bend the shoot close down on the smooth stone, while with the sharp edge of the other he hit the strained wood fibre a few blows. In this way he easily severed the stem. Cutting off the top of the sapling in the same manner, he had a bow about three feet in length; a rough, clumsy piece of wood, it is true, but resilient.

As my moccasin strings were buckskin and much stronger than Pitamakan's cow-leather ones, we used one of mine for the bowstring. We now carried the base stick and drill back from the creek into the thick timber, gathered a large bunch of birch bark and a pile of fine and coarse twigs, and made ready for this last attempt to save ourselves.

We hesitated to begin; uncertainty as to

the result was better than sure knowledge of failure, but while we waited we began to freeze. It was a solemn and anxious moment when Pitamakan set the point of the drill in the hole, made one turn of the bowstring round its centre, and held it in place by pressing down with the palm of his left hand on the tip. With his right hand he grasped the bow, and waiting until I had the shredded bark in place round the hole, he once more started the coyote prayer song and began sawing the bow forth and back, precisely the motion of a cross-cut saw biting into a standing tree.

The wrap of the string caused the drill to twirl with amazing rapidity, and at the third or fourth saw he gave a howl of pain and dropped the outfit. I had no need to ask why. The drill tip had burned his hand; when he held it out a blister was already puffing up.

We changed places, and I gathered the skirt of my capote in a bunch to protect my hand. I began to work the bow, faster and faster, until the drill moaned intermittently, like a miniature buzz-saw. In a moment or two I thought that I saw a very faint streak of smoke stealing up between my companion's fingers.

He was singing again, and did not hear my exclamation as I made sure that my eyes had not deceived me. Smoke actually was rising. I sawed harder and harder; more and more smoke arose, but there was no flame.

"Why not?" I cried. "Oh, why don't you burn?"

Pitamakan's eyes were glaring anxiously, greedily at the blue curling vapor. I continued to saw with all possible rapidity, but still there was no flame; instead, the smoke began to diminish in volume. A chill ran through me as I saw it fail.

I was on the point of giving up, of dropping the bow and saying that this was the end of our trail, when the cause of the failure was made plain to me. Pitamakan was pressing the shredded bark too tight round the drill and into the hole; there could be no fire where there was no air. "Raise your fingers!" I shouted. "Loosen up the bark!"

I had to repeat what I said before he understood and did as he was told. Instantly the bark burst into flame.

"Fire! Fire! Fire!" I cried, as I hastily snatched out the drill.

"*I-puh-kwi-is! I-puh-kwi-is!*" (It burns! It burns!) Pitamakan shouted.

He held a big wad of bark to the tiny flame, and when it ignited, carried the blazing, sputtering mass to the pile of fuel that we had gathered and thrust it under the fine twigs. These began to crackle and snap, and we soon had a roaring fire. Pitamakan raised his hands to the sky and reverently gave thanks to his gods; I silently thanked my own for the mercy extended to us. From death, at least by freezing, we were saved!

The sun was setting. In the gathering dusk we collected a huge pile of dead wood, every pieçe in the vicinity that we had strength to lift and carry, some of them fallen saplings twenty and thirty feet long. I was for putting a pile of them on the fire and having a big blaze. I did throw on three or four large chunks, but Pitamakan promptly lifted them off.

"That is the way of white people!" he said. "They waste wood and stand, half freezing, away back from the big blaze. Now we will have this in the way we Lone People do it, and so will we get dry and warm."

While I broke off boughs of feathery balsam fir and brought in huge armfuls of them, he set up the frame of a small shelter close to the fire. First, he placed a triangle of heavy sticks, so that the stubs of branches at their tops interlocked, and then he laid up numerous sticks side by side, and all slanting together at the top, so as to fill two sides of the triangle. These we shingled with the fir boughs, layer after layer, to a thickness of several feet. With the boughs, also, we made a soft bed within.

We now had a fairly comfortable shelter. In shape it was roughly like the half of a hollow cone, and the open part faced the fire. Creeping into it, we sat on the bed, close to the little blaze. Some cold air filtered through the bough thatching and chilled our backs. Pitamakan pulled off his capote and told me to do the same. Spreading them out, he fastened them to the sticks of the slanting roof and shut off the draft. The heat radiating from the fire struck them, and reflecting, warmed our backs. The ice dropped from our clothes and they began to steam; we were actually comfortable.

But now that the anxieties and excitement of the day were over, and I had time to think about other things than fire, back came my hunger with greater insistence than ever. I could not believe it possible for us to go without eating as long as Pitamakan said his people were able to fast. Worse still, I saw no possible way for us to get food. When I said as much to Pitamakan, he laughed.

"Take courage; don't be an afraid person," he said. "Say to yourself, 'I am not hungry,' and keep saying it, and soon it will be the truth to you. But we will not fast very long. Why, if it were necessary, I would get meat for us this very night."

I stared at him. The expression of his eyes was sane enough. I fancied that there was even a twinkle of amusement in them. If he was making a joke, although a sorry one, I could stand it; but if he really meant what he said, then there could be no doubt but that his mind wandered.

"Lie down and sleep," I said. "You have worked harder than I, and sleep will do you good. I will keep the fire going."

At that he laughed, a clear, low laugh of amusement that was good to hear. "Oh, I meant what I said. I am not crazy. Now think hard. Is there any possible way for us to get food this night?"

"Of course there is n't," I replied, after a moment's reflection. "Don't joke about the bad fix we are in; that may make it all the worse for us."

He looked at me pityingly. "Ah, you are no different from the rest of the whites. True, they are far wiser than we Lone People. But take away from them the things their powerful medicine has taught them how to make, guns and powder and ball, fire steels and sticks, knives and clothes and blankets of hair, take from them these things and they perish. Yes, they die where we should live, and live comfortably."

I felt that there was much truth in what he said. I doubted if any of the company's men, even the most experienced of them, would have been able to make a fire had they been stripped of everything that they possessed. But his other statement, that if necessary he could get food for us at once.

"Where could you find something for us to eat now?" I asked.

"Out there anywhere," he replied, with a wave of the hand. "Have n't you noticed the trails of the rabbits, hard-packed little paths in the snow, where they travel round through the brush? Yes, of course you have. Well, after the middle of the night, when the moon rises and gives some light, I could go out there and set some snares in those paths, using our moccasin strings for loops, and in a short time we would have a rabbit; maybe two or three of them."

How easy a thing seems, once you know how to do it! I realized instantly that the plan was perfectly feasible, and wondered at my own dullness in not having thought of it. I had been sitting up stiffly enough before the fire, anxiety over our situation keeping my nerves all a-quiver. Now a pleasant sense of security came to me. I felt only tired and sleepy, and dropped back on the boughs.

"Pitamakan, you are very wise," I said, and in a moment was sound asleep. If he answered I never heard him.

Every time the fire died down the cold awoke one or both of us to put on fresh fuel; and then we slept again, and under the circumstances, passed a very restful night.

Soon after daylight snow began to fall again, not so heavily as in the previous storm, but with a steadiness that promised a long period of bad weather. We did not mind going out into it, now that we could come back to a fire at any time and dry ourselves.

Before setting forth, however, we spent some time in making two rude willow arrows. We mashed off the proper lengths with our "anvil" and cutting-stone, smoothed the ends by burning them, and then scraped the shafts and notched them with our obsidian knives. I proposed that we sharpen the points, but Pitamakan said no; that blunt ones were better for bird shooting, because they smashed the wing bones. Pitamakan had worked somewhat on the bow during the evening, scraping it thinner and drying it before the fire, so that now it had more spring; enough to get us meat, he thought. The great difficulty would be to shoot the unfeathered, clumsy arrows true to the mark.

Burying some coals deep in the ashes to make sure that they would be alive upon our return, we started out. Close to camp, Pitamakan set two rabbit snares, using a part of our moccasin strings for the purpose. His manner of doing this was simple. He bent a small, springy sapling over the rabbit path, and stuck the tip of it under a low branch of another tree. Next he tied the buckskin string to the sapling, so that the noose end of it hung cross-wise in the rabbit path, a couple of inches above the surface of it. Then he stuck several feathery balsam tips on each side of the path, to hide the sides of the noose and prevent its being blown out of place by the wind. When a passing rabbit felt the loop tighten on its neck, its struggles would release the tip of the spring-pole from under the bough, and it would be jerked up in the air and strangled.

From camp, we went down the valley, looking for grouse in all the thickest clumps of young pines. Several rabbits jumped up ahead of us, snow-white, big-footed and black-eyed. Pitamakan let fly an arrow at one of them, but it fell short of the mark.

There were game trails everywhere. The falling snow was fast filling them, so that we could not distinguish new tracks from old; but after traveling a half-mile or so, we began to see the animals themselves, elk and deer, singly, and in little bands. As we approached a tangle of red willows, a bull, a cow, and a calf moose rose from the beds they had made in them. The cow and calf trotted away, but the bull, his hair all bristling forward, walked a few steps toward us, shaking his big, broad-horned head. The old trappers' tales of their ferocity at this time of year came to my mind, and I began to look for a tree to climb; there was none near by. All had such a large circumference that I could not reach halfway round them.

"Let's run!" I whispered.

"Stand still!" Pitamakan answered. "If you run, he will come after us."

The bull was not more than fifty yards from us. In the dim light of the forest his eyes, wicked little pig-like eyes, glowed with a greenish fire. The very shape of him was terrifying, more like a creature of bad dreams than an actual inhabitant of the earth. His long head had a thick, drooping upper lip; a tassel of black hair swung from his lower jaw; at the withers he stood all of six feet high, and sloped back to insignificant hind quarters; his long hair was rusty gray, shading into black. All this I took in at a glance. The bull again shook his head at us and advanced another step or two. "If he starts again, run for a tree," Pitamakan said.

That was a trying moment. We were certainly much afraid of him, and so would the best of the company men have been had they stood there weaponless in knee-deep snow. Once more he tossed his enormous horns;

but just as he started to advance, a stick snapped in the direction in which the cow and calf had gone. At that he half turned and looked back, then trotted away in their trail. The instant he disappeared we started the other way, and never stopped until we came to our shelter.

It was well for us that we did return just then. The falling snow was wetting the ash-heap, and the water would soon have soaked through to the buried coals. We dug them up and started another fire, and sat before it for some time before venturing out again. This experience taught us, when leaving camp thereafter, to cover the coal-heap with a roof of wood or bark.

"Well, come on! Let 's go up the valley this time, and see what will happen to us there," said Pitamakan, when we had rested.

Not three hundred yards above camp we came to a fresh bear trail, so fresh that only a very thin coating of snow had fallen since the passing of the animal. It led us to the river, when we saw that it continued on the other side up to the timber, straight toward the cave that had sheltered us. The tracks, plainly outlined in the sand at the edge of the water, were those of a black bear. "That is he, the one that gathered the leaves and stuff we slept in, and he's going there now!" Pitamakan exclaimed.

"If we only had his carcass, how much more comfortable we could be!" I said. "The hide would be warm and soft to lie on, and the fat meat would last us a long time."

"If he goes into the cave to stay, we'll get him," said Pitamakan. "If we can't make bows and arrows to kill him, we will take strong, heavy clubs and pound him on the head."

We went up the valley. Trailing along behind my companion, I thought over his proposal to club the bear to death. A month, even a few days back, such a plan would have seemed foolish; but I was fast learning that necessity, starvation, will cause a man to take chances against the greatest odds. And the more I thought about it, the more I felt like facing that bear.

I was about to propose that we go after it at once, when, with a whirr of wings that startled us, a large covey of blue grouse burst from a thicket close by, and alighted here and there in the pines and firs. We moved on a few steps, and stopped within short bow-shot of one. It did not seem to be alarmed at our approach, and Pitamakan took his time to fit one of the clumsy arrows and fire it.

Zip! The shaft passed a foot from its body, struck a limb above and dropped down into the snow. But the grouse never moved. Anxiously I watched the fitting and aiming of the other arrow.

Zip! I could not help letting out a loud yell when it hit fair and the bird came fluttering and tumbling down. I ran forward and fell on it the instant it struck the snow, and grasped its plump body with tense hands.

"Meat! See! We have meat!" I cried, holding up the fine cock.

"Be still! You have already scared all the other birds out of this tree!" said Pitamakan.

It was true. There had been three more in that fir, and now, because of my shouts, they were gone. Pitamakan looked at me reproachfully as he started to pick up the fallen arrows. Right there I learned a lesson in self-restraint that I never forgot.

We knew that there were more grouse in near-by trees, but they sat so still and were so much the color of their surroundings that we were some time in discovering any of them. They generally chose a big limb to light on, close to the bole of the tree. Finally our hungry eyes spied three in the next tree, and Pitamakan began shooting at the lower one, while I recovered the arrows for him.

Luck was against us. It was nothing, but miss, miss, miss, and as one by one the arrows grazed the birds, they hurtled away through the forest and out of sight. We were more fortunate a little farther on, for we got two birds from a small fir. Then we hurried to camp with our prizes.

I was for roasting the three of them at once, and eating a big feast; but Pitamakan declared that he would not have any such doings. "We'll eat one now," he said, "one in the evening, and the other in the morning."

We were so hungry that we could not wait to cook the first bird thoroughly. Dividing it, we half roasted the portions over the coals, and ate the partly raw flesh. Although far from enough, that was the best meal I ever had. And it was not so small, either; the blue grouse is a large and heavy bird, next to the sage-hen the largest of our grouse. After eating, we went out and "rustled" a good pile of fuel. As night came on, we sat down before the blaze in a cheerful mood, and straightway began to make plans for the future, which now seemed less dark than at the beginning of the day.

"With a better bow and better arrows, it is certain that we can kill enough grouse to keep us alive," I said.

"Not unless we have snowshoes to travel on," Pitamakan objected. "In a few days the snow will be so deep that we can no longer wade in it."

"We can make them of wood," I suggested, remembering the tale of a company man.

"But we could n't travel about barefooted. Our moccasins will last only a day or two longer. One of mine, you see, is already ripping along the sole. Brother, if we are ever to see green grass and our people again, these things must we have besides food — thread and needles, skins for moccasins, clothing and bedding, and a warm lodge. The weather is going to be terribly cold before long."

At that my heart went away down. I had thought only of food, forgetting that other things were just as necessary. The list of them staggered me — thread and needles, moccasins, and all the rest! "Well, then, we must die," I exclaimed, "for we can never get all those things!"

"We can and we will," said Pitamakan, cheerfully, "and the beginning of it all will be a better bow and some real arrows, arrows with ice-rock or flint points. We will try to make some to-morrow. Hah! Listen!"

I barely heard the plaintive squall, but he recognized it. "Come on, it's a rabbit in one of the snares!" he cried, and out we ran into the brush.

He was right. A rabbit, still kicking and struggling for breath, was hanging in the farther snare. Resetting the trap, we ran, happy and laughing, back to the fire with the prize.

After all, we ate two grouse, instead of one, that evening, burying them under the fire, and this time letting them roast long enough so that the meat parted easily from the bones.

CHAPTER V

"MY grandfather told me that this is one way that it was done," said Pitamakan, as taking a flake of obsidian in the palm of his left hand, he tapped it with an angular stone held in his right hand. "The other way was to heat the ice-rock in the fire, and then with a grass stem place a very small drop of water on the part to be chipped off."

We had been out after flints, and finding none, had brought back the pieces of obsidian that we had placed at the foot of the tree. Earlier in the morning, on visiting the snares, we had found a rabbit in each. They hung now in a tree near by, and it was good to see them there; the rabbit remaining from our first catch had been broiled for our breakfast.

Following my partner's example, I, too, tried to work a piece of the obsidian into an arrow-point. The result was that we spoiled much of the none too plentiful material. It would not chip where we wanted it to, and if we hit it too hard a blow it splintered.

Deciding now to try the fire-and-water method, we made for the purpose a pair of pincers of a green willow fork, and melted a handful of snow in a saucer-shaped fragment of rock. I was to do the heating of the obsidian and Pitamakan was to do the flaking. He chose a piece about an inch and a half long, a quarter of an inch thick, and nearly triangular in shape. One edge was as sharp as a razor; the other two were almost square-faced.

According to his directions, I took the fragment in the pincers by the sharp edge, so as to leave the rest free to be worked upon. Gradually exposing it to the heat, I held it for a moment over some coals freshly raked from the fire, and then held it before him, while with the end of a pine needle he laid a tiny drop of water near the lower corner, about a quarter of an inch back from the squared edge. There was a faint hiss of steam, but no apparent change in the surface of the rock. We tried it again, dropping the water in the same place. *Pip!* A small scale half the size of the little finger nail snapped off and left a little trough in the square edge. We both gave cries of delight; it seemed that we had hit on the right way to do the work.

A little more experimenting showed that the piece should be held slanting downward in the direction in which the flaking was to be done, for the cold water caused the rock to scale in the direction in which the drop ran. In the course of two hours the rough piece of obsidian was chipped down to a small arrow-point—one that Pitamakan's grandfather would have scorned, no doubt, but a real treasure to us.

We worked all that day making the points; when evening came we had five that were really serviceable. At sundown, the weather having cleared, we went to look at the rabbit-snares. As neither had been sprung, we moved them to a fresh place. This last storm had added a good deal to the depth of the snow; it was so much now above our knees that walking in it was hard work.

We had now before us a task almost as difficult as making the points; that is, to find suitable material for our bows and arrows. We found none that evening, but the next morning, after visiting the snares and taking one rabbit, we stumbled on a clump of service-berry treelets, next to ash the favorite bow-wood of the Blackfeet.

Back to the camp we went, got our "anvil" and hacking-stones, and cut two straight, limbless stems, between two and three inches in diameter. Next we had a long hunt through the willows for straight arrow-shafts, found them, and got some coarse pieces of sandstone from the river to use as files.

Two days more were needed for making

the bows and the arrow-shafts. The bows were worked down to the right size and shape only by the hardest kind of sandstone-rubbing, and by scraping and cutting with obsidian knives. But we did not dare to dry them quickly in the fire for fear of making the wood brittle, and they had not the strength of a really good weapon.

We made a good job of the arrows, slitting the tips, inserting the points, and fastening them in place with rabbit-sinew wrappings. For the shafts, the grouse wings provided feathering, which was also fastened in place with the sinew. Fortunately for us, the rabbit-snares kept us well supplied with meat, although we were growing tired of the diet.

Only one thing caused us anxiety now — the cords for our bows. We had to use for the purpose our moccasin strings, which were not only large and uneven, but weak. Pitamakan spoke of cutting off a braid of his hair for a cord, but on the morning after the weapons were finished, he said that in the night his dream had warned him not to do this. That settled it.

On this morning we went early to the snares and found a rabbit hanging in each. Taking the nooses along with the game to camp, we slowly dried them before the fire, for they must now serve as bowstrings. After they were dry we tested one of them, and it broke. We knotted it together and twisted it with the other to make a cord for Pitamakan's bow. That left me without one, and unable to string my bow until some large animal was killed that would furnish sinew for the purpose. I was by no means sure that the twisted and doubled cord was strong enough.

"You 'd better try it before we start out," I suggested.

"No, we must n't strain it any more than we can help," Pitamakan replied; and with that he led off down the valley.

Although the sun shone brightly, this

was the coldest day that we had yet had. Had we not worn rabbit-skins, with fur side in, for socks, we could not have gone far from the fire. The trees were popping with frost, a sign that the temperature was close to zero.

Soon after leaving camp we struck a perfect network of game tracks, some of which afforded good walking—when they went our way. For there was no main trail parallel to the river, such as the buffalo and other game always made along the streams on the east side of the Rockies. On the west side of course there were no buffalo, and probably never had been any; and to judge from the signs, the other animals wandered aimlessly in every direction.

We went ahead slowly and noiselessly, for we hoped to see some of the game lying down, and to get a close shot before we were discovered. Presently a covey of ruffed grouse, flying up out of the snow into the pines, afforded easy shots; but we dared not risk our arrows for fear of shattering the points against the solid wood. We determined thereafter always to carry a couple of blunt ones for bird shooting.

Soon after passing the grouse, I caught a glimpse of some black thing that bobbed through the snow into a balsam thicket. We went over there and came to the trail of a fisher, the largest member of the weasel family. As I had often seen the large, glossy black pelts of these animals brought into the fort by Indians and company trappers, I was anxious to get a close view of one alive. I looked for it farther along in the snow; but Pitamakan, who was gazing up into the trees, all at once grasped my arm and pointed at a small red-furred creature that, running to the end of a long bough, leaped into the next tree.

"Huh! Only a squirrel!" I said. But I had barely spoken when, hot after it, jumped the fisher, the most beautiful, agile animal that I had ever seen. It was considerably larger than a house cat.

We ran, or rather waddled, as fast as we could to the foot of the fir, barely in time to see the fisher spring into the next tree, still in pursuit of the squirrel. The latter, making a circle in the branches, leaped back into the tree over our heads. The fisher was gaining on it, and was only a few feet behind its prey when, seeing us, it instantly whipped round and went out of that tree into the one beyond, and from that to another, and another, until it was finally lost to sight.

"Oh, if we could only have got it!" I cried.

"Never mind, there are plenty of them here, and we 'll get some before the winter is over," said my companion.

Although I had my doubts about that, I made no remark. Pitamakan was promising lot of things that seemed impossible,—needles and thread, for instance. "Let 's go on," I said. "It is too cold for us to stand still."

We came now to the red willow thicket

where the bull moose had frightened us. There a barely perceptible trough in the new-fallen snow marked where he and his family had wandered round and retreated, quartering down the valley.

"They are not far away, but I think we had better not hunt them until we have two bows," Pitamakan remarked.

Just below the red willows we saw our first deer, a large, white-tail doe, walking toward the river, and stopping here and there to snip off tender tips of willow and birch. We stood motionless while she passed through the open timber and into a fir thicket.

"She is going to lie down in there. Come on," said Pitamakan.

He started toward the river and I followed, although I wondered why he did n't go straight to the deer trail. Finally I asked him the reason, and right there I got a very important lesson in still-hunting.

"All the animals of the forest lie down facing their back trail," he explained. "Some-

We had sneaked into the thicket for perhaps fifty yards when, for all his care, Pitamakan grazed with his shoulder a snow-laden branch of balsam, and down came the whole fluff of it. I saw the snow farther on burst up as if from the explosion of a bomb, and caught just a glimpse of the deer, whose tremendous leaps were raising the feathery cloud. It had only a few yards to go in the open; but Pitamakan had seen it rise from its bed, and was quick enough to get a fair shot before it disappeared.

"I hit it!" he cried. "I saw its tail drop! Come on."

That was a certain sign. When a deer of this variety is alarmed and runs, it invariably raises its short, white-haired tail, and keeps swaying it like the inverted pendulum of a clock; but if even slightly wounded by the hunter, it instantly claps its tail tight against its body and keeps it there.

"Here is blood!" Pitamakan called out, pointing to some red spots on the snow. They were just a few scattering drops, but I consoled myself with thinking that an arrow does not let out blood like a rifle-ball because the shaft fills the wound. We soon came to the edge of the fir thicket. Beyond, the woods were so open that we could see a long way in the direction of the deer's trail. We dropped to a walk, and went on a little less hopefully; the blood-droppings became more scattering, and soon not another red spot was to be seen — a bad sign.

At last we found where the deer had ceased running, had stopped and turned round to look back. It had stood for some time, as was shown by the well-trodden snow. Even here there was not one drop of blood, and worst of all, from this place the deer had gone on at its natural long stride.

"It is useless for us to trail her farther," said Pitamakan dolefully. "Her wound is only a slight one; it smarts just enough to keep her traveling and watching that we don't get a chance for another shot."

I felt bad enough, but Pitamakan felt worse, because he thought that he should have made a better shot.

"Oh, never mind," I said, trying to cheer him. "There are plenty of deer close round here, and it is a long time until night. Go ahead. We'll do better next time."

"I am pretty tired," he complained. "Perhaps we had better go to camp and start out rested to-morrow."

I had not thought to take the lead and break trail a part of the time; of course he was tired. I proposed to do it now, and added that it would be a good plan to walk on the ice of the river and look carefully into the timber along the shores for meat of some kind.

"You speak truth!" he exclaimed, his face brightening in a way that was good to see. "Go ahead; let 's get over there as quick as possible."

In a few minutes we were back on the ice, where he took the lead again. And now for the first time since leaving camp — except for a few minutes after the shot at the deer — I felt sure that with so much game in the valley we should kill something. On the smooth, new ice, our moccasins were absolutely noiseless; we were bound to get a near shot. Inside of half an hour we flushed several coveys of grouse, and saw an otter and two mink; but there were so many tracks of big game winding round on the shore and in and out of the timber that we paid no attention to the small fry.

It was at the apex of a sharp point, where the river ran right at the roots of some big pines, that we saw something that sent a thrill of expectation through us; the snow on a willow suddenly tumbled, while the willow itself trembled as if something had hit it. We stopped and listened, but heard nothing. Then nearer to us the snow fell from another bush; from another closer yet, and Pitamakan made ready to shoot just as a big cow elk walked into plain view and stopped, broadside toward us, not fifty feet away.

"Oh, now it is meat, sure," I thought, and with one eye on the cow and the other on my companion, I waited breathlessly.

For an instant Pitamakan held the bow motionless, then suddenly drew back the cord with a mighty pull, whirled half round on the slippery ice and sat down, with the bow still held out in his left hand. From each end of it dangled a part of the cord!

That was a terrible disappointment. Such a fair chance to get a big fat animal lost, all because of that weak bowstring! The elk had lunged out of sight the instant Pitamakan moved. He sat for a moment motionless on the ice, with bowed head, a picture of utter dejection. Finally he gave a deep sigh, got up slowly and listlessly, and muttered that we had better go home.

"Wait! Let's knot the cord together," I proposed. "That may have been the one weak place in it."

He shook his head in a hopeless way and started upstream, but after a few steps halted, and said, "I have no hope, but we'll try it."

The cord had been several inches longer than was necessary, and after the knot was made it was still long enough to string the bow. When it was in place again, Pitamakan gave it a half pull, a harder one, then fitted an arrow and drew it slowly back; but before the head of the shaft was anywhere near the bow, *frip!* went the cord, broken in a new place. We were done for unless we could get a new and serviceable cord! Without a word Pitamakan started on and I followed, my mind all a jumble of impossible plans.

We followed the winding river homeward in preference to the shorter route through the deep snow. The afternoon was no more than half gone when we arrived at the little shelter, rebuilt the fire, and sat down to roast some rabbit meat.

"We can't even get any more rabbits," I

said. "There are so many knots in our strings that a slip-noose can't be made with them."

"That is true, brother," said Pitamakan, "so we have but one chance left. If there is a bear in that cave across the river we have got to kill him."

"With clubs?"

"Yes, of course. I told you that my dream forbids the cutting of my hair, and so there is no way to make a bowstring."

"Come on! Come on!" I said desperately. "Let's go now and have it over."

We ate our rabbit meat as quickly as possible, drank from the spring, and by the help of the indispensable "anvil" and our cutting-stones, we got us each a heavy, green birch club. Then we hurried off to the river. Although much snow had fallen since we had seen the black bear's tracks there, its trail was still traceable up through the timber toward the cave.

CHAPTER VI

WELL, we took up the dim trail on the farther side of the river and followed it through the timber toward the cave at the foot of the cliff, but I, for my part, was not at all anxious to reach the end of it. Midway up the slope I called to Pitamakan to halt.

"Let's talk this over and plan just what we will do at the cave," I proposed.

"I don't know what there is to plan," he answered, turning and facing me. "We walk up to the cave, stoop down, and shout, 'Sticky-mouth, come out of there!' Out he comes, terribly scared, and we stand on each side of the entrance with raised clubs, and whack him on the base of the nose as hard as we can. Down he falls. We hit him a few more times, and he dies."

"Yes?" said I. "Yes?"

I was trying to remember all the bear stories that I had heard the company men and the Indians tell, but I could call to mind no story of their attacking a bear with clubs.

"Yes? Yes what? Why did you stop? Go on and finish what you started to say."

"We may be running a big risk," I replied. "I have always heard that any animal will fight when it is cornered."

"But we are not going to corner this bear. We stand on each side of the entrance; it comes out; there is the big wide slope and the thick forest before it, and plenty of room to run. We will be in great luck if, with the one blow that we each will have time for, we succeed in knocking it down. Remember this: We have to hit it and hit hard with one swing of the club, for it will be going so fast that there will be no chance for a second blow."

We went on. I felt somewhat reassured, and was now anxious to have the adventure over as soon as possible. All our future depended on getting the bear. I wondered whether, if we failed to stop the animal with our clubs, Pitamakan would venture to defy his dream, cut off a braid of his hair, and make a bow-cord.

Passing the last of the trees, we began to climb the short, bare slope before the cave, when suddenly we made a discovery that was sickening. About twenty yards from the cave the trail we were following turned sharply to the left and went quartering back into the timber. We stared at it for a moment in silence. Then Pitamakan said, dully:—

"Here ends our bear hunt! He was afraid to go to his den because our scent was still there. He has gone far off to some other place that he knows."

The outlook was certainly black. There was but one chance for us now, I thought, and that was for me to persuade this red brother of mine to disregard his dream and cut off some of his hair for a bow-cord. But turning round and idly looking the other way, I saw something that instantly drove this thought from my mind. It was a dim trail along the foot of the cliff to the right of the cave. I grabbed Pitamakan by the arm, yanked him round, and silently pointed at it. His quick eyes instantly discovered it, and he grinned, and danced a couple of steps.

"Aha! That is why this one turned and went away!" he exclaimed. "Another bear was there already, had stolen his home and bed, and he was afraid to fight for them. Come on! Come on!"

We went but a few steps, however, before he stopped short and stood in deep thought. Finally he turned and looked at me queerly, as if I were a stranger and he were trying to learn by my appearance what manner of boy I was. It is not pleasant to be stared at in that way. I stood it as long as I could, and then asked, perhaps a little impatiently, why he did so. The answer I got was unexpected:—

"I am thinking that the bear there in the

cave may be a grizzly. How is it? Shall we go on and take the chances, or turn back to camp? If you are afraid, there is no use of our trying to do anything up there."

Of course I was afraid, but I was also desperate; and I felt, too, that I must be just as brave as my partner. "Go on!" I said, and my voice sounded strangely hollow to me. "Go on! I will be right with you."

We climbed the remainder of the slope and stood before the cave. Its low entrance was buried in snow, all except a narrow space in the centre, through which the bear had ploughed its way in, and which, since its passing, had partly filled. The trail was so old that we could not determine whether a black or a grizzly bear had made it.

But of one thing there could be no doubt: the animal was right there in the dark hole, only a few feet from us, as was shown by the faint wisps of congealed breath floating out of it into the cold air. Pitamakan, silently stationing me on the right of the entrance, took his place at the left side, and motioning me to raise my club, shouted, "*Pahk-si-kwo-yi, sak-sit!*" (Sticky-mouth, come out!)

Nothing came; nor could we hear any movement, any stir of the leaves inside. Again he shouted; and again and again, without result. Then, motioning me to follow, he went down the slope. "We'll have to get a pole and jab him," he said, when we came to the timber. "Look round for a good one."

We soon found a slender dead pine, snapped it at the base where it had rotted, and knocked off the few scrawny limbs. It was fully twenty feet long, and very light.

"Now I am the stronger," said Pitamakan, as we went back, "so do you handle the pole, and I will stand ready to hit a big blow with my club. You keep your club in your right hand, and work the pole into the cave with your left. In that way maybe you will have time to strike, too."

When we came to the cave, I found that his plan would not work. I could not force the pole through the pile of snow at the entrance with one hand, so standing the club where I could quickly reach it, I used both hands. At every thrust the pole went in deeper, and in the excitement of the moment I drove it harder and harder, with the result that it unexpectedly went clear through the obstructing snow and on, and I fell headlong.

At the instant I went down something struck the far end of the pole such a rap that I could feel the jar of it clear back through the snow, and a muffled, raucous, angry yowl set all my strained nerves a-quiver. As I was gathering myself to rise, the dreadful yowl was repeated right over my head, and down the bear came on me, clawing and squirming. Its sharp nails cut right into my legs. I squirmed as best I could under its weight, and no doubt went through the motions of yelling; but my face was buried in the snow, and for the moment I could make no sound.

Although I was sure that a grizzly was upon me and that my time had come, I continued to wiggle, and to my great surprise, I suddenly slipped free from the weight, rose up, and toppled over backward, catching, as I went, just a glimpse of Pitamakan fiercely striking a blow with his club. I was on my feet in no time, and what I saw caused me to yell with delight as I sprang for my club. The bear was kicking and writhing in the snow, and my partner was showering blows on its head. I delivered a blow or two myself before it ceased to struggle.

Then I saw that it was not a grizzly, but a black bear of no great size. Had it been a grizzly, I certainly, and probably Pitamakan, too, would have been killed right there.

It was some little time before we could settle down to the work in hand. Pitamakan had to describe how he had stood ready, and hit the bear a terrific blow on the nose as it came leaping out, and how he had followed it up with more blows as fast as he could swing his club. Then I tried to tell how I had felt, crushed under the bear and expecting every instant to be bitten and clawed to death. But words failed me, and, moreover, a stinging sensation in my legs demanded my attention; there were several gashes in them from which blood was trickling, and my trousers were badly ripped. I rubbed the wounds a bit with snow, and found that they were not so serious as they looked.

The bear, a male, was very fat, and was quite too heavy for us to carry; probably it weighed two hundred pounds. But we could drag it, and taking hold of its fore paws, we started home. It was easy to pull it down the slope and across the ice, but from there to camp, across the level valley, dragging it was very hard work. Night had fallen when we arrived, and cold as the air was, we were covered with perspiration.

Luckily, we had a good supply of wood

on hand. Pitamakan, opening the ash-heap, raked out a mass of live coals and started a good fire. Then we rested and broiled some rabbit meat before attacking the bear. Never were there two happier boys than we, as we sat before our fire in that great wilderness, munched our insipid rabbit meat and gloated over our prize.

The prehistoric people no doubt considered obsidian knives most excellent tools; but to us, who were accustomed only to sharp steel, they seemed anything but excellent; they severely tried our muscles, our patience, and our temper. They proved, however, to be not such bad flaying instruments. Still, we were a long time ripping the bear's skin from the tip of the jaw down along the belly to the tail, and from the tail down the inside of the legs to and round the base of the feet. There were fully two inches of fat on the carcass, and when we finally got the hide off, we looked as if we had actually wallowed in it. By that time, according to the Big Dipper, it was past midnight, but Pitamakan would not rest until he had the back sinews safe out of the carcass and drying before the fire for early use.

It is commonly believed that the Indians used the leg tendons of animals for bow-cords, thread, and wrappings, but this is a mistake; the only ones they took were the back sinews. These lie like ribbons on the outside of the flesh along the backbone, and vary in length and thickness according to the size of the animal. Those of a buffalo bull, for instance, are nearly three feet long, three or four inches wide, and a quarter of an inch thick. When dry, they are easily shredded into thread of any desired size.

Those that we now took from the bear were not two feet long, but were more than sufficient for a couple of bow-cords. As soon as we had them free, we pressed them against a smooth length of dry wood, where they stuck; and laying this well back from the fire, we began our intermittent night's sleep, for, as I have said, we had to get up frequently to replenish the fire.

The next morning, expecting to have a fine feast, I broiled some of the bear meat over the coals, but it was so rank that one mouthful was more than enough; so I helped Pitamakan finish the last of the rabbit meat. He would have starved rather than eat the meat of a bear, for to the Blackfeet the bear is "medicine," a sacred animal, near kin to man, and therefore not to be used for food.

Killing a grizzly was considered as great a feat as killing a Sioux, or other enemy. But the successful hunter took no part of the animal except the claws, unless he were a medicine-man. The medicine-man, with many prayers and sacrifices to the gods, would occasionally take a strip of the fur to wrap round the roll containing his sacred pipe.

Pitamakan himself was somewhat averse to our making any use of the black bear's hide, but when I offered to do all the work of scraping off the fat meat and of drying it, he consented to sleep on it once with me, as an experiment, and if his dreams were good, to continue to use it.

I went at my task with good will, and was half the morning getting the hide clean and in shape to stretch and dry. Pitamakan meanwhile made two bow-cords of the bear sinew. First he raveled them into a mass of fine threads, and then hand-spun them into a twisted cord of the desired length; and he made a very good job of it, too. When he had stretched the cords to dry before the fire, he sharpened a twig of dry birch for an awl, and with the rest of the sinew, repaired our badly ripped moccasins. At noon we started out to hunt, and on the way dragged the bear carcass back to the river and across it into the big timber, where later on we hoped to use it for bait.

This day we went up the river, walking noiselessly on the ice. From the start we felt confident of success; for not only were our bow-cords as good as we could desire, but the bows were now in fine condition, having dried out and become more stiff, yet springy. Since, during the latter part of the night, more snow had fallen, we could distinguish fresh game tracks from old ones. And now that there was snow on the ice, we naturally expected to see where the hoofed game had been crossing the river ; they seldom venture out on smooth ice, from fear of slipping and injuring themselves.

The first game we saw were a number of ruffed grouse standing in a row at the edge of a strip of open water, to take their daily drink. They walked away into the willows at our approach, and from there flew into the firs, where we knocked down four of them with our blunt-headed bird arrows. I got only one, for of course I was not so good a marksman with bow and arrow as my partner, who had used the weapon more or less since he was old enough to walk.

Burying the grouse in the snow at the edge of the shore, we went on, and presently came to the place where several elk had crossed to the north side of the river, browsed among a bordering patch of red willows, and then gone into the thick firs. We followed them, not nearly so excited now that we had trustworthy weapons as we had been on the previous hunt. When we came near the firs, which covered several acres of the bend in the river, Pitamakan sent me round to enter the farther side and come through the patch toward him, while he took his stand close to the place where the band had entered.

"You need n't come back carefully," he said to me. "Make all the noise you can — the more the better; then they will come running out here on their back trail, and I 'll get some good shots. You 'd better give me one of your real arrows, for you will probably not get a chance even for one shot at them."

That left me with only one arrow with an obsidian point, but nevertheless I determined to do my best to get an elk. As Pitamakan had remarked about himself, I, too, felt the sun power strong within me that morning and looked for success. With that feeling, call it what you will, — all old hunters will understand what I mean, — I was not at all surprised, a short time after entering the firs, to see, as I was sneaking along through them, a big bull elk astride a willow bush that he had borne down in order to nip the tender tips.

He was not fifty feet from me, and no doubt thought that the slight noise which he heard was made by one of his band. He could not see me at first, because of a screen of fir branches between us, and he had not looked up when I made the final step that brought me into the open. But when I raised the bow, he jerked his head sidewise and gathered himself for a jump.

He was not so quick as I. The strength of a giant seemed to swell in my arms; I drew the arrow sliding back across the bow almost to the head with a lightning-like pull, and let it go, *zip!* deep into his side through the small ribs.

Away he went, and I after him, yelling at the top of my voice to scare the herd toward Pitamakan, if possible. I saw several of them bounding away through the firs, but my eyes were all for the red trail of the bull. And presently I came to the great animal, stretched across a snow-covered log and breathing its last; for the arrow had pierced its lungs.

"*Wo-ke-hai! Ni-kai-nit-ah is-stum-ik!*" (Come on! I have killed a bull!) I yelled.

And from the far side of the firs came the answer: "*Nis-toah ni-mut-uk-stan!*" (I have also killed!)

That was great news. Although it was hard for me to leave my big bull even for a moment, I went to Pitamakan, and found that he had killed a fine big cow. He had used three arrows, and had finally dropped her at the edge of the river.

We were so much pleased and excited over our success that it was some time before we could cease telling how it all happened and settle down to work. We had several fresh obsidian flakes, but as the edges soon grew dull, we were all the rest of the day in getting the hides off the animals and going to camp with the meat of the cow. The meat of my bull was too poor to use, but his skin, sinews, brains, and liver were of the greatest value to us, as will be explained.

"There is so much for us to do that it is hard to decide what to do first," said Pitamakan that night.

It was long after dark, and we had just gathered the last of a pile of firewood and sat ourselves down before the cheerful blaze.

"The first thing is to cook a couple of grouse, some elk liver, and hang a side of elk ribs over the fire to roast for later eating," I said, and began preparing the great feast.

After our long diet of rabbits, it was a

feast. We finished the birds and the liver, and then sat waiting patiently for the fat ribs to roast to a crisp brown as they swung on a tripod over the fire. I was now so accustomed to eating meat without salt that I no longer craved the mineral, and of course my companion never thought of it. In those days the Blackfeet used none; their very name for it, *is-tsik-si-pok-wi* (like fire tastes), proved their dislike of the condiment.

"Well, let us now decide what we shall do first," Pitamakan again proposed. "We need new moccasins, new leggings and snowshoes. Moreover, we need a comfortable lodge. Which shall be first?"

"The lodge," I answered, without hesitation. "But how can we make one? What material can we get for one unless we kill twenty elk and tan the skins? That would take a long time."

"This is a different kind of lodge," he explained. "When you came up the Big River you saw the lodges of the Earth People? Yes. Well, we will build one like theirs."

On the voyage up the Missouri with my uncle I had not only seen the lodges of the Earth People (Sak-wi Tup-pi), as the Blackfeet called the Mandans, but I had been inside several of them, and noted how warm and comfortable they were. Their construction was merely a matter of posts, poles, and earth. We agreed to begin one in the morning, and do no hunting until it was done.

The site that we chose for the lodge was a mile below camp and close to the river, where two or three years before a fire, sweeping through a growth of "lodge-pole" pines, had killed thousands of the young, slender trees. In a grove of heavy firs close by we began the work, and as every one should know how to build a comfortable house without the aid of tools and nails, I will give some details of the construction.

In place of the four heavy corner posts which the Mandans cut, we used four lowcrotched trees that stood about twenty feet apart in the form of a square. In the crotches on two sides of the square we laid as heavy a pole as we could carry, and bolstered up the centre with a pile of flat rocks, to keep it from sagging. On the joists, as these may be called, we laid lighter poles side by side, to form the roof. In the centre we left a space about four feet wide, the ends of which we covered with shorter poles, until we reduced it to a hole four feet square.

The next task was to get the poles for the sides. These we made of the proper length by first denting them with sharp-edged stones and then snapping them off. They were slanted all round against the four sides, except for a narrow space in the south side, which we left for a doorway. Next we thatched the roof and sides with a thick layer of balsam boughs, on top of which we laid a covering of earth nearly a foot deep. This earth we shoveled into an elk hide with elk shoulder blades, and then carried each load to its proper place. Lastly, we constructed in the same manner a passageway six or eight feet long to the door.

All this took us several days to accomplish, and was hard work. But when we had laid a ring of heavy stones directly under the square opening in the roof for a fireplace, made a thick bed of balsam boughs, and covered it with the bearskin, put up an elkskin for a door, and sat us down before a cheerful fire, we had a snug, warm house, and were vastly proud of it.

"Now for some adventure," said Pitamakan, as we sat eating our first meal in the new house. "What say you we had best do?"

"Make some moccasins and snowshoes," I replied.

"We can do that at night. Let us —"

The sentence was never finished. A terrible booming roar, seemingly right overhead, broke upon our ears. Pitamakan's brown face turned an ashy gray as he sprang up, crying:

"Run! Run! Run!"

CHAPTER VII

OUT into the snow we ran, while nearer and nearer sounded that terrific roaring and rumbling; it was as if the round world was being rent asunder. Pitamakan led the way straight back from the river toward the south side of the valley, and we had run probably two hundred yards before the noise ceased as suddenly as it had begun. We were quite out of breath, and it was some time before I could ask what had happened.

"Why, don't you know?" he said. "That was a great piece of the ice cliff on the mountain across there. It broke off and came tearing down into the valley. Trees, boulders, everything in its way were smashed and carried down. I thought that it was going to bury our lodge."

Pitamakan wanted to make an early start in the morning to view the path of the avalanche, but I insisted that we stay at home and work hard until the things that we needed so much were finished. I had my way.

Ever since the day of the elk killing, we had kept one of the big hides in the river in order to loosen the hair. In the morning we brought it into the lodge, and laying it over a smooth, hard piece of driftwood, grained it with a heavy elk rib for a graining-knife. It was very hard work. Although we sharpened an edge of the rib with a piece of sandstone and kept it as sharp as possible, we had to bear down on it with all our strength, pushing it an inch or two at a time in order to separate the hair from the skin. Taking turns, we were half a day in finishing the job.

We cut the hide into two parts. Of these, we dried one, and cut the other into webbing-strings for snowshoes — tedious work with our obsidian knives. As soon as the half hide was dry, I rubbed elk brains and liver well into it, and then, rolling it up, laid it away for a couple of days until the mixture could neutralize the large amount of glue that is in all hides. After that operation, I spent half a day in washing the hide and then rubbing and stretching it as it dried. I had then a very good piece of elk leather, — so-called "buckskin," — enough for four pairs of moccasins.

These Pitamakan and I made very large, so that they would go over the rabbit-skins with which we wrapped our feet as a protection from the cold. Our needle for sewing them was a sharp awl made from a piece of an elk's leg bone; the thread was of elk sinew.

O-wam (shape of eggs) is the Blackfoot name for snowshoes. Those that we made were neither shaped like an egg nor like anything else. The bows were of birch, and no two were alike, and the webbing was woven on them in a way to make a forest Indian laugh. Neither Pitamakan's people nor the other tribes of the plains knew anything about snowshoes except in a general way, and I had never seen a pair. All things considered, however, we did a fairly good job. If the shoes were heavy and clumsy, at least they were serviceable, for they sank only a few inches in the snow when we tested them.

The evening we finished this work another snowstorm came on, which lasted two nights and a day, and forced us to postpone our hunt. We employed the time in improving the interior of the lodge by building a heavier stone platform for the fire, one that would give off considerable heat after we went to sleep.

In order to create a draft for the fire, we were forced to admit some air through the doorway, and this chilled us. Finally, I remembered that I had seen in the Mandan lodges screens several feet high, put between the doorway and the fire, in order to force the cold air upward.

We made one at once of poles, backed with earth, and then, building a small fire, sat down on our bed to see how it worked; no more cold air swept across the floor, and we were absolutely comfortable. But in the night, although the stones gave out some heat, we were obliged to replenish the fire as soon as it died down. What we needed in order to have unbroken sleep was bedding. Pitamakan said that one animal here, the white mountain goat, had a warmer, thicker coat of fur than the buffalo. We determined to get some of the hides and tan them into soft robes.

The morning after the storm broke clear and cold, but my partner refused to go up into the high mountains after goats.

"We must put it off and do something else to-day," he said. "I had a very bad dream last night—a confused dream of a bear and a goat, one biting and clawing me, and the other sticking its sharp horns into my side. Now either that is a warning not to hunt goats to-day, or it is a sign that the bearskin that we are sleeping on is bad medicine. This is not the first bad dream that I have had since lying on it."

"My dreams have all been good since we began sleeping on it," I said.

"Then use it by yourself; I shall not sleep on it again."

"Oh, dreams don't mean anything!" I exclaimed. "White people pay no attention to them."

"That is because your gods give you different medicine from that our gods give us," he said, very seriously. "To us is given the dream; in that way our gods show us the things we may and may not do. Do not speak lightly of it, lest you bring harm to me."

I had sense enough to heed his wish; never afterward, either by word or look, did I cast even a shadow of doubt upon his beliefs. For that reason, largely, we got along together in perfect harmony, as all companions should.

As there was in his dream nothing about other animals, we put on our snowshoes and started out to hunt and set traps in the valley.

At odd moments we had been making triggers of different sizes for deadfalls, and now had fifteen ready to use. They were of the "figure 4" pattern; more complicated than the two-piece triggers, but more sure of action. Having with the small ones set deadfalls for marten, fisher, and mink, we went on up the river to the carcasses of the bear and the bull elk. We found that both had been almost entirely eaten by wolverenes, lynxes, and mountain lions. Having built at each of these places a large deadfall, we weighted the drop-bars so heavily with old logs that there could be no escape for the largest prowler once he seized the bait.

By the time we had the last of the triggers baited and set up and the little pen built behind the drop-bar, night was coming on, and we hurried home. We had seen many tracks of deer, elk, and moose, but had been too busy to hunt any of them. As we neared the lodge, another snowstorm set in, but that did not disturb us; in fact, the more snow the better, for with deep snow the hoofed game of the valley would be unable to escape us. We could choose the fat does and cows for our winter's meat. The bucks and bulls were already poor, and the others would lose flesh rapidly once they were obliged to "yard," that is, to confine themselves to their hard-beaten trails in the limited area of a willow patch.

It was a heavy snow that fell in the night, and the next morning snowshoeing was good. As Pitamakan had had no bad dreams, and the sun was shining in a clear sky, we started out for a goat hunt. After climbing the mountain-side opposite the lodge for some time, we came to a series of ledges, whence we obtained a fine view of the country which we were living in. The mountain which we were on was high and very steep. Not far below its summit was the big ice field, terminating at the edge of a cliff, from which a great mass had tumbled, and started the avalanche that had frightened us.

Turning to the east and pointing to the backbone of the range, Pitamakan told me to notice how absolutely white it all was except the perpendicular cliffs, where snow could not lie. There was no question but that the snow was a great deal deeper up there than where we were.

I thought that there was a longing in Pitamakan's eyes as he gazed at the tremendous wall of rock and snow that separated us from the plains and from our people, but as he said nothing, I kept quiet. For myself, I felt that I would give anything, suffer any hardships, if I could only get once more to Fort Benton and my uncle. True, we now had a comfortable lodge and plenty of elk meat, weapons for killing game, snowshoes for traveling, and the outlook for more comforts was favorable. But for all that, the future was very uncertain; there were many things that might prevent our ever reaching the Missouri; all nature was arrayed against us, and so was man himself.

Pitamakan roused me from my reverie by a tap on the shoulder.

"I can see no goat signs here above us," he said, "but look over there at the ledges well up on the next mountain to the east. Do you see the fresh trails?"

I did. In the smooth, glittering snow they were startlingly distinct in their windings and turnings from clump to clump of the pines on the rocky ledges. None of the animals that made them were in sight, but that was not strange; as they were of practically the same color as the snow, we could not see them at that distance except when they happened to get in front of the dark pines or rock. Although the distance over there was not more than a mile in a straight line, a cut gorge between the two mountains obliged us to return to the river before making the ascent, which more than doubled the distance.

After striking the river, we followed it up past the mouth of the gorge, past three of the deadfalls set near the shore. The first one held a fine, large, dark-furred marten, its body nipped across the shoulders and crushed by the drop-bar. Taking the little victim out, and hanging it in a tree, we reset the trap. The next deadfall was unsprung. The third, one of the big falls, was down, and we hurried as fast as we could to see what it held.

"A lynx," I ventured.

"A wolverene," Pitamakan guessed.

We were both wrong. Pinned down by the neck was a big mountain lion, to us the most valuable of all the animals of the forest. The Blackfeet, as well as the Crows and Gros Ventres, prized the skins very highly for use as saddle-robes — we could get at least four horses for this one. Taking such a prize made us feel rich. Leaving it in the fall until our return, we turned off from the river and began the ascent of the mountain in high spirits.

For a time the going was good, although

increasingly difficult. After we had passed through the big timber, the mountain became more and more steep, until it was impossible for us to go farther on snowshoes. Taking them off, we wallowed up through the deep snow from ledge to ledge, keeping away from the clumps of stunted pine as much as possible, for in them the snow lay deepest and was most fluffy.

The weather was bitterly cold, but we were warm enough, even perspiring from our exertions. Much as we needed to stop and rest at frequent intervals, it was impossible to do so, for the instant we halted we began to shiver. More than once we were on the point of giving up the hunt, but each time the thought of what a few goat hides meant to us strengthened our legs to further endeavor.

I never envied a bird more than I did one that I saw that day. A Clark's crow it was, raucous of voice and insolent, that kept flying a short distance ahead of us and lighting on the pines, where it pretended to pick kernels out of the big cones. If we could only fly like that, I kept thinking, within a moment's time we could be right on the goats.

Strange as it may seem, there was more bird life on that bleak, cold height than in the forest below. One variety of small, sweet singers, flying all round us in large flocks, was especially numerous. I wondered what they could be. Long years afterward an ornithologist told me that they were gray-crowned finches — arctic birds that love the winter cold and are happiest in a snow-drift.

We saw, too, many chattering flocks of Bohemian waxwings, also visitors from the arctic regions. Most interesting of all were the ptarmigan, small, snow-white grouse with jet-black eyes, bill, and toes. Never descending to the valleys, either for food or shelter, they live on the high, bare mountains the year round. They are heavily feathered clear to the toes, so that their feet cannot freeze; and at night, and by day, too, in severe weather, instead of roosting in the dwarf pines they plunge down into soft snow, tunnel under the surface for several feet, and then tramp a chamber large enough to sit in. These birds were very tame, and often allowed us to get within fifteen or twenty feet of them before flying or running away. Some were saucy and made a great fuss at our approach, cocking up their tails and cackling, and even making a feint of charging us.

At last we came walking out on a ledge that ended at the side of a big gouge in the mountain, and on the far verge of it saw a goat, a big old fellow, sitting at the edge of a small cliff. It was sitting down on its haunches, just as a dog does. Should you see a cow, a sheep, or any herbivorous animal do that, you would think his position extremely ludicrous. In the case of the goat, because of its strange and uncouth shape, it is more than ludicrous; it is weird. The animal has a long, broad-nosed head, set apparently right against its shoulders; a long, flowing beard hangs from its chin; its withers are extremely high, and its hams low, like those of the buffalo. Its abnormally long hair flutters round its knees like a pair of embroidered pantalets, and rises eight or ten inches in length above the shoulders. The tail is short, and so heavily haired that it looks like a thick club. Its round, scimitar-shaped black horns rise in a backward curve from the thick, fuzzy coat, and seem very small for the big, deep-chested animal.

The goat was almost as new to Pitamakan as to me.

"What is the matter with it?" he exclaimed. "Do you think it is sick, or hurt?"

"He looks as if he felt very sad," I replied.

And truly the animal did look very dejected, its head sunk on its brisket, its black eyes staring vacantly at the valley far below, as if it were burdened with all the pains and sorrows of the ages.

We were so interested in watching it that at first we did not see the others, thirteen in all, scattered close round on the little ledges above him. Some were standing, others lying down. One big old "billy" lay under a low-branched dwarf pine, and now and then would raise its head, bite off a mouthful of the long, coarse needles, and deliberately chew them. We had come out in plain view of the band, and now wondered that they had not seen us and run away.

"Let's back up step by step until we are in the shelter of the pines back there, then look out a way to get to them," Pitamakan proposed.

On starting to do so, we found that the goats had seen us all the time. Two or three of them turned their heads and stared at us with apparent curiosity; the old billy at the edge of the cliff gave us one vacant stare, and resumed his brooding; the others paid no attention to our movements. Unquestionably they had never seen man before, and did not consider us enemies because we were not four-legged, like the beasts that preyed upon them. So instead of backing cautiously, we turned and walked into the little clump of pines, and beyond them to a deep gutter, where we began the difficult task of stalking the animals. We had to climb for several hundred yards to a broad ledge, follow it for perhaps twice that distance, and then work our way, as best we could, straight down to the goats.

That was a terrible climb. As the angle of the mountain was such that the climb would have been difficult on bare rock, you can imagine how hard it was to go up in the deep snow. Using our snowshoes for shovels and taking the lead in turn, we fought our way through, upward, inch by inch. More than once a mass of snow gave way above our gouging, and swept us down a few feet or a few yards. Once Pitamakan was buried so deep in it that I was obliged to dig him out; he was gasping for breath by the time I uncovered his head.

On the ledge the going was so level that we wore our snowshoes a part of the way across, and then, wading to a point directly above the goats, we began the descent. That was easy. Straight ahead of us the mountain dropped in a series of little shelves, or cliffs, down which we could easily climb. Stopping when we thought we were near to the goats, we strung our bows and fitted arrows to them. As I was a poor shot, I took but one arrow, to be used only in an emergency. Pitamakan carried the other four.

In a few moments we struck a deep and well-packed goat trail that meandered along a shelf thirty, and in places fifty feet wide. Here and there were clumps of dwarf pine and juniper that prevented our seeing very far ahead, and Pitamakan gave me the sign to look sharp for the game.

A moment later, as we followed the trail

round some pines, we came face to face with a big billy-goat. The instant that he saw us he bristled up his hair and came for us. Did you ever see a wild pig prance out for a fight? Well, that is the way that goat came at us — head down and prancing sidewise. I don't know whether we were more surprised or scared; probably scared. The sight of those round, sharp black horns made our flesh creep; indeed, the whole aspect of the uncouth animal was terrifying.

Coming at us head on, there was little chance for an arrow to do any damage to him.

"Run out that way!" Pitamakan cried, as he gave me a push. "I'll go this way!"

There was not any running about it; we waddled to one side and the other from the cañon-like trail out into the deep snow, and it was remarkable what progress we made. As I said, the goat came prancing toward us, not jumping full speed, as he might have done, so that we had plenty of time to get out of the trail.

When he came opposite he seemed undecided what to do next. We did not give him time to make up his mind. Pitamakan let fly an arrow, while I stood ready to shoot if need be. But Pitamakan's shaft sped true; the old billy flinched and humped himself, threw up his head with a pitiful, silly expression of surprise, and dropped in his tracks. We waded back into the trail and examined our prize; such heavy, thick, long hair and fleece I had never seen on any other animal. At the base of the sharp horns were black, warty, rubber-like excrescences. "Smell them!" Pitamakan bade me, and I did. They gave off an exceedingly rank odor of musk.

Pitamakan now pulled out the arrow; it had evidently pierced the heart. He proposed that we go after the band and kill as many as possible; we needed at least four large, or six small skins for a good bed-robe.

"Well, come on, lead the way," I said.

He held up his hand, and I could see his

eyes grow big as if from fear. "What is it?" I asked.

He did not answer, but stood anxiously looking this way and that, and soon I, too, heard the faint, remote droning noise that had alarmed him. We looked at the mountain above us, and at others near and far, but there was nowhere any sign of an avalanche.

The droning noise became louder and deeper, filling us with dread all the more poignant because it was impossible to determine the cause.

"The old medicine-men told the truth!" said Pitamakan. "These mountains are no place for the Blackfeet. The gods that dwell here are not our gods, and they do strange and cruel things to us plains people when they get the chance."

I had nothing to say. We listened; the droning grew louder; it seemed all about us, and yet we could see nothing unusual.

"Come on!" Let's get away from here!" Pitamakan cried.

CHAPTER VIII

"WHERE shall we go?" I asked. "This noise seems to come from everywhere and nowhere."

I looked up at the top of the mountain which we were on, and saw a long streak of snow extending eastward from it like an immense pennant.

"Look! It is nothing but the wind that is making that noise!" I exclaimed. "See how it is driving the snow up there!"

"Yes," Pitamakan agreed. "But listen. The sound of its blowing does not come from there any more than from elsewhere. It comes from every direction up there in the blue."

We could now see snow flying from the tops of the mountains on the opposite side of the valley. In a few moments the whole summit of the range was lost in a vast haze of drifting, flying snow. But where we were there was only a gentle breeze from the west, which did not increase in force. I remembered now that in winter, when fierce northwest winds blew across the plains, the summit of the Rockies was always hidden by grayish-white clouds. It was a strange sensation to hear the drone of a terrific wind and not feel it, and I said so.

"Everything is strange in this country," my partner said, dully. "Here Wind-Maker lives; and many another of the mountain and forest gods. We have to make strong medicine, brother, to escape them."

This was the first of the terrific winter winds that blow across the Northwest plains. Many a time thereafter we heard the strange roaring sound that seemed to come from nowhere in particular; but down in the valley, and even high up on the sides of the mountains, near the lodge, there was never more than a gentle breeze. Pitamakan was always depressed when we heard the strange roaring, and it made me feel nervous and apprehensive of I knew not what.

We waded and slid and fell down to the next ledge, and there, working our way to the edge, we saw some of the goats right beneath us. There were seven of them,—old "nannies," two kids, and "billies" one and two years old,—all in a close bunch not more than twenty feet below us. Instead of running, they stood and stared up at us vacuously, while their concave faces seemed to heighten their expression of stupid wonder.

Pitamakan shot one of the nannies. At the same time I drew my bow on one of the goats, but on second thought eased it, for I might waste a precious arrow. I had to use all my will power in denying myself that chance to add another animal to my list of trophies.

Pitamakan was not wasting any time: *Zip! Zip! Zip!* he sped his remaining arrows, reached out for one of mine, and shot it just as an old nannie, awaking to the fact that something was wrong with her kindred, started off to the left at a lumbering gallop, more ungainly and racking than that of a steer. Here was success, indeed! I was so excited that I went aimlessly from one to another of the goats, feeling of their heavy coats and smooth, sharp horns.

Having dressed the animals, we dragged them from the ledges out on the steep slide, where we fastened them one to another in a novel way. Making a slit down the lower joint of a hind leg, we thrust a fore leg of the next animal through it, — between tendon and bone, — then slit the fore leg in the same manner, and stuck a stick in it so that it could not slip out. We soon had all five animals fastened in line, and then taking the first one by the horns, we started down.

The deep snow was now a help instead of a hindrance; for it kept our tow of game from sliding too fast down the tremendously steep incline. Knowing that we were likely to start an avalanche, we kept as close to the edge of the timber as we could. Even so, I had the feeling which a man has while walking on thin ice over deep water. I tried to push cautiously through the snow, and looked back anxiously whenever the game in a particularly steep place came sliding down on us by the mere pull of its own weight.

Pitamakan was less apprehensive. "If a slide starts, we can probably get out of it by making a rush for the timber," he said. "Anyhow, what is to be will be, so don't worry."

We came safe to the foot of the slide, but had time to skin only one goat before dark; it was slow work with our obsidian knives. As we could not safely leave the others unprotected from the prowlers during the night, we laid them side by side on a heap of balsam boughs, where the air could circulate all round them, and Pitamakan hung his capote on a stick right over them, in order that the sight and odor of it might prevent any wandering lion, lynx, or wolverene from robbing us. To go without his capote in such cold weather was certainly a sacrifice on Pitamakan's part.

If I am asked why we took pains to lay the game on boughs, the answer is that, although any one would think that snow would be a natural refrigerator, the opposite is the case, for freshly killed animals will spoil in a few hours if they are buried in it.

To keep from freezing, Pitamakan hurried on to camp, while I followed slowly with the goatskin and head. There was not time to take the lion or marten from the deadfalls.

When I got to the lodge, Pitamakan had a fire burning and the last of the cow elk ribs roasting over it. We were wet to the skin, of course, but that did not matter. Off came our few garments, to be hung a short time over the fire and then put on again. How cheerful and restful it was to stretch out on our balsam beds and enjoy the heat after the long day's battle with snow and precipitous mountain-sides!

The next day, and for many days thereafter, we had much work to keep us busy. We skinned the goats, tanned the hides into soft robes, and sewed them together in the form of a big bag, with the fur side in. The night on which we crawled into it for the first time was a great occasion. On that night, for the very first time since leaving the Blackfoot camp, we slept perfectly warm and without waking with shivers to rebuild the fire.

The deadfalls also took a great deal of our time. Every night some of them were sprung, and we found from one to three or four valuable fur animals under the drop-bars. It was a tedious job to skin them and properly stretch the pelts to dry, but for all that, we loved the work and were proud of the result. Here and there in the lodge a few marten, fisher, wolverene, and lynx skins were always drying, and in a corner the pile of cured peltries was steadily growing. Three of them were of mountain lions.

During this time much more snow fell; it was fully six feet deep in the woods when the last of the elk hams was broiled and eaten. For a day or two we subsisted on goat meat, although the best of it had a slight musky odor and flavor. As Pitamakan said, it was not real food.

As our bows were not nearly so strong as they looked, my partner was always wishing for glue, so that we might back them with sinew. There was material enough for glue, but there was nothing to make it in.

"The Mandans made pots of earth," I said to him one day. "Perhaps we can make one that will stand fire and water."

Out we went along the river to look for clay. At the first cut-bank that we came to I gouged off the snow that thinly coated its perpendicular side, and lo! there was a layer of clay six inches thick between two layers of gravel. We broke out several large flat chunks of the stuff, — it was frozen, of course, — and carried it to the lodge. There, breaking it into fine pieces and thawing it, we added a small amount of water, and worked it into a stiff paste of the right consistency, as we thought, for moulding.

Pitamakan, always artistic, fashioned a thin bowl like those that he had seen in the Mandan village, while I made mine an inch thick, with a capacity of not more than two quarts. When we baked them in the coals, mine cracked, and Pitamakan's fell to pieces.

That was discouraging; evidently the clay was not of the right consistency. I worked up another portion of clay with less water, while my partner added even more water than before to his batch. We each soon had a bowl fashioned and put to bake. In a few minutes the one which Pitamakan had made fell to pieces, but mine, which was thick and clumsy in shape, seemed to stand the heat well. I gradually increased the fire round it, and after keeping the blaze up for a long time, I allowed the fire at last to die out gradually. The bowl turned out fairly well; for although it had one crack in the side, it was dark red in color, and gave a substantial ring when we tapped it with a stick.

However, we took no chances of a mishap by moving it. We plastered the crack with fresh clay, and then, putting into it nearly a quart of water, an elk hoof and a couple of goat hoofs, we rebuilt the fire just close enough to make the mixture simmer, and adding more water from time to time during the day, patiently awaited results.

"*Ai-y!* It is real glue!" Pitamakan exclaimed that evening, after dipping a stick in the mess and testing it with his fingers. We were quite excited and proud of our success. Softening the four elk sinews in the hot glue, Pitamakan then plastered a pair of them on each bow. The place where the ends overlapped at the centre, he bound with a sinew wrapping.

Of course the bows were unstrung when

the backing was put on, and as soon as the work was done, we laid them away from the fire, that they might dry slowly. In the morning, the first thing, after crawling out of our fur nest, we strung and tested them, and found that the backing had more than doubled their strength and elasticity. Now we were ready to hunt our winter meat, and after a hurried breakfast of musky goat steak, we started in quest of the game.

Not since the day of the goat hunt had we seen any tracks of moose, elk, or deer. Pitamakan said that he had heard that the deer went from the high mountains down toward the lake of the Flatheads to winter, and that we need not expect to see any more of them. But he added that it did not matter, for other game would yard close round the lodge.

Taking a zigzag course and examining every red willow patch along our route, we went down the valley. As it was a stinging cold day, we had our hands tucked up in the sleeves of our capotes, and our bows and arrows under our arms, for as yet we had no mittens. Our legs suffered, too, from need of new coverings.

The first game that we saw was an otter, fishing in a dark pool at the foot of a rapid. He would crawl out on the ice fringing it, sit still for a moment, sniffing the air and looking sharp for any enemy, and then make a sudden dive. We watched him until he had brought up a big trout and had begun to eat it, when we turned away without the animal seeing us. Except at close range, the otter's eyesight is poor, but he has a keen nose and sharp ears. Later we intended to set a deadfall for him, if by any means we could catch fish to bait it.

A mile or more below the lodge we came to a deep, hard-packed trail, which wound and branched in every direction through a big red-willow thicket, which we guessed to be a moose yard. In many places the willows had been browsed off as far out from the paths as the animals could stretch their necks. Here and there were large, hard-packed circular depressions in the snow where they had lain down to rest and sleep, always, I imagine, with one of their number on the watch for any prowling mountain lion.

We went down through the centre of the yard, although we had some difficulty in crossing the deep trails on our snowshoes. Soon we sighted the game — two cow moose, two calves, and two yearlings. The instant that they saw us the old lead cow trotted away down the trail, leading the others, and then by turning into every successive left-hand fork, tried to circle round behind us. When we headed her off, she turned and tried to circle round us in the other direction. Then Pitamakan and I separated, and in that way drove the little band steadily ahead of us, until it reached the lower end of the yard.

There, with a tremendous leap, the old cow broke out of the yard into the fresh snow, and the way she made it fly behind her reminded me of the stern wheel of a Missouri River steamboat beating up spray. All the others followed her until we came close, when all but her calf wheeled in the new path and rushed back for the yard.

They were so close to us that we might almost have touched them. Pitamakan shot an arrow deep between the ribs of the cow, and by a lucky aim I put my one arrow into the calf behind her. Both of them fell, but the two yearlings, scrambling over their bodies, escaped into the yard.

We went on in pursuit of the other cow and her calf. The strength that she displayed in breaking her way through six feet of snow was wonderful. For at least three hundred yards she went faster than we could go on our web shoes, but after that she gave out rapidly, and finally stopped altogether.

When we came close to her, she plunged back past the calf and stood awaiting us, determined to protect it to the last All the hair on her shoulders and back was ruffed and bristling forward, while her eyes blazed with anger, although there was also in them the look of terror and despair. When we got close to her, she rushed at us. We had to do some lively scrambling to keep out of her way. But she soon tired, and then while I attracted her attention, Pitamakan slipped round on the other side of her. As his bow-cord twanged, she dropped her head, and the light almost instantly went out of her eyes. The poor calf met the same fate a moment later. It was cruel work, but as necessary as it was cruel; we killed that we might live.

There remained the two yearlings, and I proposed that we spare them. Pitamakan looked at me with surprise.

"What! Let them go?" he exclaimed. "And many winter moons yet before us? Why, brother, you talk foolishly! Of course we must kill them. Even then we may not have enough meat to last until spring."

So we chased them also out into deep snow, and did as he said. By the time we had one calf skinned we were obliged to go home and gather the night's wood.

The next day we skinned the rest of the animals, cut up the meat, and hung it in trees, whence it could be packed home from time to time. Two of the hides we put to soak in the river, preparatory to graining and tanning them. The others we stretched on frames and allowed to freeze dry, after which we laid them on our couch.

During the short days we tended the dead-falls, skinned and stretched what fur was trapped in them, packed in meat and hung it beside the lodge, and tanned the two hides. Having done the tanning successfully, we went into the tailoring business. Pitamakan cut pieces of proper shape from the big, soft skins, but in the work of sewing I did my share. After three or four evenings' work, we were the proud wearers of new shirts, new leggings, and new mittens.

Our earthen pot fell to pieces the day after we had made glue in it. That was a serious loss, for we had intended to boil meat in it. Roasted meat is good, but does not do so well as a steady diet. The Indians of the North regard boiled meat as we regard bread, that is, as the staff of life. Pitamakan, who craved it more than I, determined, now that we had plenty of hides, to use a part of one for a kettle. From one of the yearling moose hides he cut a large, round piece, soaked it in the river until it was soft, and then sewed the edge in pleats to a birch hoop about two feet in diameter, so as to make a stiff-rimmed bag about as deep as it was wide. With a strip of hide he suspended it from a pole in the lodge roof.

Next he set several clean stones in the fire to heat, and put some rather finely cut meat in the bag with two quarts of water. When the rocks were red-hot, he dropped them one by one into the bag, and pulled them out to reheat as fast as they cooled. In this way the meat was boiled. Such was the ancient way of cooking it before the white traders brought pots and kettle into the North country.

The meat was not cooked long, only long enough, in fact to change its color, and was really more nutritious than it would have been had it been stewed a long time. We enjoyed that first meal of it with keen relish, and thereafter ate more boiled than roasted meat.

As the winter snows settled and hardened, we saw more and more trails of otter along the river, where they traveled from one open hole to another to do their fishing, and one day we began our campaign against them by going fishing ourselves. Our tackle consisted of a sinew cord and loop several feet long, tied to a long, slender pole.

In the first open pool that we looked into there were numerous trout and suckers; of course we tried first to snare the trout. We soon learned, however, that it could not be done, for they would not allow the loop to come nearer than five or six inches to their heads, but always drifted downstream from it in a tantalizing manner.

Next, trying the suckers, big, reddish-black fellows of two pounds' weight, we found them easy to snare. They lay as if they were half dead, their bellies close to the bottom, and never moved when the loop drifted down round their heads, thinking, no doubt, that it was but a piece of passing water-grass. When the noose was just behind the gills, we gave the pole a sharp yank, and up came the fish, wriggling and flapping, helpless in the grip of the tightened cord.

After we caught three of them, we spent the rest of the morning setting a deadfall at each of three pools where the otters were working. But for some time afterward we got no otters; of all animals they are the shyest and most difficult to trap. It was not until all traces of the man scent had died out that one was finally lured by the sucker bait, and was killed by the fall-bar.

As time passed, we set more and more deadfalls up and down the valley, so many that finally we could not make the round of them all in one day. One morning we would attend to those lying east of the lodge, and the next morning visit those to the west of it. The farthest one to the west was at least seven miles away, and for some unknown reason more fur came to it than to any of the others; we seldom visited it without finding a marten or a fisher. Pitamakan called it the *nat-o-wap-i kyak-ach-is* — medicine-trap, as the words may be freely translated. *Nat-o-wap-i* really means "of the sun" — "sun-power."

As we approached this deadfall one day, when we had taken nothing from the other traps except a marten that a passing fisher had maliciously torn to shreds, Pitamakan began the coyote prayer song, because, as he said, something had to be done to bring us better luck.

We soon saw the deadfall, noticed that the bar was down, and hurried eagerly forward to see what it held, while my partner sang louder than ever. On coming to it, we found a fine, black, fluffy-furred fisher; whereupon Pitamakan raised his hand and began chanting a prayer of thanks to the gods.

Meanwhile I saw, a little farther on, a trail in the snow which excited my interest, and I impatiently waited for him to finish his devotions to call his attention to it.

"Look! There's the trail of a bear!" I said, although it seemed odd to me that a bear should be wandering round in the dead of winter.

We hurried over to it. What we saw made us stare wildly round with fright, while we quickly strung our bows. It was the trail of a man on long, narrow web shoes—an Indian, of course, and therefore an enemy. The trail was fresh, too, apparently as fresh as our own. And but a moment before, Pitamakan had been singing at the top of his voice!

CHAPTER IX

CROSSING the valley from south to north in front of us, the snowshoe trail disappeared, a hundred yards away, in a clump of pines. The Indian, brushing against a branch, had relieved it of its weight of snow, and its dark green foliage stood out in sharp contrast with the prevailing white. There was a chance that he might still be in that thicket.

"We must know if he is there," said Pitamakan. "Though he did n't hear us we must still know whence this enemy came, and why, and where he is going."

We began by going cautiously round the pines. From a distance, we could see the trail coming out of them on the farther side and going on straight to the river, where the water fell in cascades over a wide series of low, broken reefs. From there the trail followed the edge of the open water down past the last of the falls, and then showed plain on the frozen river as far as we could see.

Venturing now to follow it to the cascades, we learned at a glance, on arriving there, why the lone traveler had come into our peaceful valley. At the edge of the water the snow was all trampled down, and the prints of bare feet in it showed that the man had been wading in the river. Scattered on the packed snow were several fragments of dark green rock, one of which Pitamakan picked up and examined.

"This is what he came after," he said. "It is pipestone and very soft. Both the Kootenays and the Flatheads make their pipes of it because it is so easily worked into shape."

"Where do you think he came from?" I asked.

"From the camp of his people. These mountain Indians winter down along their big lake. Very little snow falls there, and horse-feed is always good."

"Well, if he came from down there, why

do we find his trail to this place coming straight across the valley from the south?"

"Ah, that is so!" Pitamakan exclaimed. "Come on! We must find out about that."

We took the man's back trail, and, passing our deadfall, paused to note how plainly it could be seen from several points along the way. It was a wonder that he had noticed neither the deadfall nor our hard-packed, snowshoe trail.

"The gods were certainly good to us!" my partner exclaimed. "They caused him to look the other way as he passed."

The back trail led us straight to the foot of the steep mountain rising from the valley. There, in several places, the snow was scraped away to the ground, where evidently the man had searched for the pipestone ledge that was probably exposed somewhere near. Failing to find it, he had been obliged to go to the river and wade to the place where it again cropped out. His trail to the side hill came straight up the valley.

We certainly had something to think and talk about now—and also to worry about. Others of the enemy might come after pipestone, and there was our trail running straight to the place. Going back to the deadfall, we took out the fisher, but did not reset the trap; for we determined not to go thereafter within several miles of the pipestone falls. Another heavy snowfall would pretty much obliterate our trail, and we prayed that it would soon come. From that day, indeed, our sense of peace and security was gone.

Sitting within the lodge, we always had the feeling that the enemy might be close by, waiting to shoot us when we stepped outside. On the daily rounds of our traps we were ever watching places where a foe might be lying in wait. Pitamakan said that the only thing for us to do was to make strong medicine. Accordingly, he gave our bearskin to the sun; he lashed it firmly in the fork of a tree, and made a strong prayer to the shining god to guard us from being ambushed by the enemy.

Although we had long since lost track of the days of the week, we agreed in thinking that the discovery of the man's trail took place in "the moon before the moon when the web-feet come"; or, as the white man would say, in February. At the end of the next moon, then,—in March,—spring would come on the plains. Up where we were, however, the snow would last much longer—probably until May. Pitamakan said that we must leave the valley long before then, because with the first signs of spring the deer would be working back into the high mountains, and the Kootenays would follow them.

"How can we do that when, as you say, the pass cannot be crossed until summer?" I asked.

"There is another pass to the south of us," he replied, "the Two Medicine pass. There is no dangerous place anywhere along it."

"Then we can easily get out of here!" I exclaimed. "Let us start soon."

He shook his head. "No," he said. "We can't go until the snow melts from the low country where the Kootenays and Flatheads winter. We have to go down there to make our start on the Two Medicine trail."

"Why so?" said I, in surprise. "Why can't we go straight south from here until we strike it?"

He laughed grimly.

"Between us and the trail lie many cañons and many mountains that none but the birds can cross. Besides, along each stream is a trail used by these Indians in their hunts up toward the backbone of the range, which is like the trail that crosses over to the Two Medicine. I could not recognize the right one when we came to it, and we should follow up one after another, and wear ourselves out. I remember some landmarks only where the right trail leaves the lake and enters the heavy timber, and from that place we have to start. Also, we have to start from there on bare ground; for if we started on the snow, our trail would be seen and followed, and that would be the end for us."

"Well, then, let 's go up and look at the summit of our pass," I proposed. "It may not be so bad as you think. Perhaps we can find some way to cross the dangerous place."

He objected that we should waste our time, but I kept urging that we must overlook no possible chance to escape to the plains, until finally I persuaded him. One bright morning we put on our snowshoes and started. As the going was good on the deep, settled snow, we were not long in covering the distance to the Salt Springs. Up and down the mountainside, all round them, was a perfect network of goat trails in the snow, and here and there were large and small groups of the strange, uncouth animals, some lying down, some sitting and staring dejectedly off into space, while still others were cropping lichens from wind-swept, rocky walls. Although several of them were less than three hundred yards away, they paid no attention to us.

After watching some that were feeding on the cliff wall, where they looked as if they were pasted to it, we came to the conclusion that they could travel where a bighorn would certainly fall and be dashed to pieces. One old billy-goat was almost human in the way in which he got over difficult places. After standing on his hind legs and gathering all the lichen within reach he concluded to ascend to the next shelf. Since there was not room for him to back away for a leap, he placed his forefeet over the edge, and drew himself up on to it — exactly as a man draws himself up by the sheer muscular strength of his arms.

Not far beyond the springs, we left the last of the timber and began the ascent of the summit proper, and soon came into the zone of terrific winds; but fortunately for us, there was scarce a breath stirring that day. The snow was so hard-packed by the wind that when we removed our snowshoes, our moccasined feet left no impressions in it. The rocky slopes facing the northwest were absolutely bare, while those pitching the other way lay buried under drifts from five to fifty feet and more in depth.

Late in the afternoon we came to the west end of the pass, having made twice as good time in the ascent as we had in the descent in the autumn with horses. I needed but one glance at the place to be convinced that it was impassable. The steep slide where my horse and I had so nearly been lost was buried deep in snow; towering above it were heavy, greenish, concave drifts of snow clinging to the knife-edge wall and likely to topple over at any moment. Our weight might, and probably would, start an avalanche rushing down the slide and off into abysmal space. We stood in the trail of several goats, which had ventured out on the slide for a few yards, abruptly turned and retraced their steps.

"Even they feared to cross," said Pitamakan. "Come on! Let's go home."

I was so disappointed that I had not a word to say on the way down. We reached the lodge late in the night, made sure that no one had been near it during our absence, and after building a good fire and eating some roast meat, crawled into our fur bag, nearly worn out. It had been a long, hard day.

At this time our catch of fur began to decrease rapidly. It is my belief that the predatory as well as the herbivorous animals never stray very far from the place where they are born.

A case in point is that of an old grizzly bear, whose trail could not be mistaken because he had lost a toe from his left front foot. Every three weeks he crossed the outlet of the Upper St. Mary's Lake, wandered up into the Red Eagle Valley, swung round northward along the back-bone of the Rockies to the Swift Current Waters, and thence down across the outlet again. Observation of other animals also leads me to believe that they all have their habitual rounds. If this is so, it explains why it was that our deadfalls held fewer and fewer prizes for us, until finally three or four days would pass without our finding even a marten to reward us for our long, weary tramps.

The days now grew noticeably longer and warmer, until finally snow-shoeing was impossible after nine or ten o'clock in the morning. The warm sun turned the snow into large, loose, water-saturated grains which would give way every few steps and let us down clear to the ground, often in places where the snow was so deep that we stood, so to speak, in a greenish well from which we had to look straight up to see the sky. It was very difficult to get out of such places.

Toward the end of our stay we did most of our tramping in the early morning, when the snow was covered with so hard a crust by the night's frost that it would hold us up without snowshoes.

One evening we heard the distant cry of wild geese. That was our signal for departure. We made a last round of the deadfalls, sprung each one that was set, and the next day made up two bundles of the peltries that we were to take with us. There were in all sixty-one marten, ten fisher, seventeen mink, five wolverene, one mountain-lion, eight lynx, and two otter skins. Fortunately, there was little weight in all that number, and we bound them so compactly that there was little bulk. A quantity of moose meat, cut into thin sheets and dried, made up the rest of our pack. Nor did we forget the fire-drill and a small, hard piece of birch wood that had been seasoning by the fire all the winter for a drill base.

The goatskin sleeping-bag was too heavy to take along; it would have added much to our comfort, of course, but there was now no night cold enough to be very disagreeable so long as we could have fire, and of that we were assured. However, Pitamakan did not intend that the bag should be wasted; almost the last thing that he did was to make an offering of it to the sun. Lashing the bundle in a tree, he prayed that we might survive all perils by the way, and soon reach the lodges of our people.

At sundown we ate our last meal in the lodge and enjoyed for the last time its cheerful shelter. Somehow, as we sat by the fire, we did not feel like talking. To go away and leave the little home to the elements and the prowlers of the night was like parting forever from some near and dear friend.

We waited several hours, until the frost hardened the snow; then putting on the snowshoes and slinging the packs, we started away down the valley. There was certainly a lump in my throat as I turned for a last look at the lodge, with the smoke of its fire curling up from it and beckoning us back to rest and sleep.

Until midnight the stiffening crust occasionally broke and let us down; but after that time it became so hard that, taking off our snowshoes and slinging them to the packs, we made remarkable time down the valley.

After passing the pipestone falls, we entered country new to us, where the valley became much wider. Every mile or two a branch came into the river, which we were obliged to ford, for the ice had gone out of the streams. It was no fun to remove moccasins and leggings, wade through the icy water, and then put them on in the snow on the other side.

For several weeks avalanches had been thundering down the mountain-sides all round us, and this night they seemed more frequent than ever. Once one tore its way to the valley just behind us. Not an hour later, Pitamakan's pack-thong broke, and let his bundle down into the snow. As we stopped to retie it, there came the rumbling of an avalanche, apparently right over our heads.

I thought that it would strike the valley not far below us. "Come! Get up!" I cried. "Let's run back as fast as we can!"

"Not so! We must run the other way. Can't you hear? It is going to strike either where we are, or close behind us," Pitamakan answered; and grasping my arm, he tried to make me go forward with him.

"Can't you hear it there?" I shouted, taking hold of him in my turn and pulling the other way. "It is coming down right where we stand, or not far below here!"

And thus we stood while the dreadful noise increased, until it seemed as if the world was being rent wide open. There was a confusion of thunderous sound — the grinding of rocks and ice, the crashing and snapping of great trees. The avalanche came nearer with teriffic speed, until finally it filled all the region round with such a deafening noise that it was impossible even to guess where it would sweep down into the valley.

We ran a few steps upstream, then as many more back, and finally stood trembling, quite uncertain which way to fly. But only for a moment; just ahead of us the great forest trees began to leap out and downward from the steep mountain-side, and then the mass of the avalanche burst into the flat and piled up a hundred feet deep before us—a dirty ridge of wrecked mountain-side that extended away across the valley to the river. There was a last rumble and cracking of branches as it settled, and then all was still.

"You see that I was right," I said. "It did strike below us."

"Yes, you heard better than I did," my partner admitted, "but that is not what saved us. I am sure that the gods caused the pack-thong to break and stop us; otherwise we should have been right in the path of the slide."

Re-slinging our packs, we climbed the rough mass of the slide, round and over big boulders, ice blocks, and tree trunks, through piles of brush and broken branches. At the apex of the heap Pitamakan reached down, pulled something from the earth-stained snow, and passed it to me. It was the head and neck of a mountain goat, crushed almost flat, the flesh of which was still warm.

"You see what would have happened to us if my pack-thong had not broken," he said grimly.

"It must be that many goats perish in this way," I remarked.

"Yes, and also many bighorn," he said. "I have heard the old hunters say that the bears, when they first come out in the spring, get their living from these slides. They travel from one to another, and paw round in search of the dead animals buried in them."

At daylight we entered an open park where we could see back toward the summit. There was no doubt that we had traveled a long way during the night, for the mountain opposite our abandoned lodge looked twenty miles distant. The valley here was fully a mile wide, and the mountains bordering it were covered with pines clear to the summit. They were not more than a thousand feet high, and the western rim of them seemed not more than fifteen miles away. We believed that from where they ended the distance could not be great to the lake of the Flatheads.

Down here the snow was only about four feet deep, less than half the depth of it where we had wintered. The air became warm much earlier in the morning than it did up there. Using the snowshoes now, as the crust was getting weak, we kept going, although very tired. During the two hours that we were able to travel after sunrise, we passed great numbers of elk, and not a few moose, and when, finally, the snow grew spongy and obliged us to stop for the day, we were plainly within the deer range, for both white-tail and mule-deer were as plentiful as jack-rabbits are in certain parts of the plains.

We stopped for our much-needed rest on a bare sandbar of the river, and with bow and drill started a little fire and roasted some dry meat. The sun shone warm there, and after eating, we lay down on the sand and slept until almost night.

Starting on again as soon as the snow crusted, we traveled the rest of the night without any trouble, and soon after day-break suddenly passed the snow-line and stepped into green-sprouting grass. The summer birds had come, and were singing all round us. A meadow-lark, on a bush close by, was especially tuneful, and Pita-makan mocked it:

"*Kit-ah-kim ai-siks-is-to-ki!*" (Your sister is dark-complexioned!) he cried gleefully. "Oh, no, little yellow-breast, you make a mistake. I have no sister."

We were in the edge of a fine prairie dotted with groves of pine and cottonwood. The land sloped gently to the west. I thought that it could not be far in that direction to the big lake, but Pitamakan said that it was way off to the southwest, perhaps two days' journey from where we were. Sud-denly he fell on his knees and began with feverish haste to dig up a slender, green-leaved plant.

"It is camass!" he cried, holding it up and wiping the earth from the white, onion-shaped root. "Dig! Dig! See, there are plenty of them all round. Eat plenty of them. They are good."

So they were; crisp, starchy, and rather sweet. After our winter-long diet of meat, they were exactly what our appetites craved and our systems needed. We made a meal of them right there. For once hunger got the better of our caution. Laying down our pack and snowshoes, we dug up root after root, all the time moving out into prairie farther and farther from the edge of the timber.

"Come on! Let 's get our packs and hide somewhere for the day," I said finally. "I am filled with these things to the neck."

"Oh, wait a little; I want a few more," my partner answered.

Just then a band of deer burst out of a cottonwood grove about five hundred yards to the west of us, and as we sat staring and wondering what had startled them, three Indians came riding like the wind round one side of the grove, and four more appeared on the other side, in swift pursuit of the animals.

CHAPTER X

"DON'T you move!" Pitamakan exclaimed.

He spoke just in time, for I was on the point of springing up and running for the timber. The game — they were muledeer, which are not fleet runners, like the white-tail — came bouncing awkwardly toward us, while the Indians gained on them perceptibly. Never before had I felt that I was a giant; but as I sat there in the short grass of the open prairie, I felt as if my body was actually towering into the sky. I instinctively tried to make myself of smaller size. All my muscles quivered and contracted so tensely that the feeling was painful. "Oh, come!" I cried. "Can't you see that they —"

"Be still!" Pitamakan broke in. "The wind is from us to them. The deer will soon turn. Our one chance is to sit motionless. They haven't seen us yet."

The deer came steadily toward us, jumping awkwardly and high. They were now less than four hundred yards away, and although the wind was increasing, they gave no sign of having scented us.

"They must turn soon," Pitamakan said. "But if they don't, and you see that the Indians are coming for us, string your bow. Let us fight our best until our end comes."

That had been my thought. I had two of our five obsidian-pointed arrows. If worse came to worst, I hoped that I should be able to speed them swift and true. Now the deer were less than three hundred yards from us, and I gave up all hope that they would turn. To me the Indians seemed to be staring straight at us instead of at the animals.

I had started to reach for my bow and arrows, which lay on the ground beside me, when the deer did turn, suddenly and sharply to the right. The pursuers, turning also, almost at the same time, gained considerably on them. I realized that we had not been discovered.

The leading hunter now raised his gun and fired. The hornless old buck at the head of the band sharply shook his head, and holding it askew as if the bullet had stung it, swerved to the right again, directly away from us. The herd followed him, while the hunters again made a short cut toward them and began shooting. Their backs were now to us.

"Run! Run for the timber!" my partner commanded; and grabbing my bow and arrows, I followed him, faster, probably, than I had ever run before. It was a hundred yards or more to the timber. As we neared it, I began to hope that we should get into its shelter unseen. Behind us the hunters kept shooting at the deer, but neither of us took time to look back until we came to our packs, and paused to lift them and the snowshoes.

At that very moment the war-cry of the

enemy was raised, and we knew that they had discovered us. We looked, and saw that they were coming our way as fast as their horses could lope. And how they did yell! There was menace in those shrill staccato yelps.

"We must leave the furs. Just take your snowshoes and come on," said Pitamakan, and I grabbed them up and followed him.

It was only a few yards back in the timber to the snow-line. Upon reaching it, I threw down my shoes, stuck my toes into the loops, and was starting on without fastening the ankle-thongs, when my partner ordered me to tie them properly. It seemed to me that my fingers had never been so clumsy.

We stepped up on the snow, and found that the crust was still strong enough to bear our weight, although it cracked and gave slightly where the centre of the poor webbing sagged under our feet. At the edge of the prairie the timber was scattering; but back a short distance there were several dense thickets, and back of them again was the line of the heavy pine forest. We made for the nearest thicket, while the yells of the enemy sounded nearer and louder at every step we took.

It was easy to guess when they came to the fur packs, for there was a momentary stop in the war-cries as they loudly disputed over the possession of them. Then, abandoning their horses, they began shooting at us as they advanced into the snow, through which they broke and floundered at almost every step.

The advantage was now all with us, provided we were not hit. Once I stopped behind a tree for an instant and looked back. Three of the men had not tried to come on over the snow, but standing at the edge of it, loaded and fired as fast as possible. The others were doing their best to advance over the crust, and had our plight not been so desperate, I should have laughed to see them. They stepped gingerly, teetering along with open mouths and arms outspread, and sometimes the crust would bear their weight for three or four paces, and so increase their confidence that they would quicken their speed, only to break through and sink waist-deep.

I pushed a flap of my old capote out from the tree as far as I could with the bow, in the hope of drawing their fire; but, finding that they were not to be caught by any such ruse, I hurried on. Then several bullets came so close to me that I could feel the wind from them; one struck a tree which I was passing, and flicked off bits of bark, which stung my left cheek and cut the lobe of my left ear. When the enemy saw me raise my hand to my face, they yelled with triumph, and Pitamakan turned to see what had happened.

"Go on! It is nothing!" I called out.

At that instant another shot was fired, and I thought that I heard my partner give a little cry of pain; but he did not flinch, and continued on as rapidly as before. When I came where he had been, however, I saw that his trail was bloody, and I feared the worst, for

I well knew that even with a death-wound he would keep on bravely to the very end. The rest of the run to the thicket was like some terrible dream to me, for I expected that every step he made would be his last. But finally he passed into the screen of young evergreens, and a moment later I was beside him, asking how badly he was hurt.

"It is only only a flesh-wound here," he answered, gripping the inner part of his left thigh. "Come on, we mustn't stop."

As the enemy could no longer see us, we made our way to the line of big timber without fear of their bullets. They gave a few last yells as we went into the thicket, and shouted some words at us, which of course we could not understand. And then all was still.

Without a word, Pitamakan went on and on up the steep mountain-side, and I sadly followed him. Soon, coming to an opening in the timber, we stepped out into it, until we could get a good view of the plain below.

The Indians were riding back to where they had chased the deer. Soon they dismounted and began skinning two that they had killed. We removed our snowshoes and sat down on them. Pitamakan let down his legging and washed his wound with snow; the bullet had split open the skin for a length of several inches, but fortunately, had not torn the muscles. As soon as the wound was washed and dry, I went over to a balsam fir and gathered the contents of three or four blisters, which he smeared all over the raw place. In a few minutes he said that the pungent, sticky stuff had stopped the burning of the wound.

We were two sad boys that morning. The loss of the furs, for which we had worked so hard all winter, was not easy to bear. Every few minutes Pitamakan would cry out to his gods to punish the thieves, and my heart was as sore against them as his. With the fur packs we had lost also our fire-drill and socket piece.

"But that doesn't matter," Pitamakan

said. "We have good bows and can make a drill at any time. Perhaps we shall never again have any use for one!"

"How so? Are we never to eat again? Shall we not need fire of nights to keep us warm?" I asked.

"Maybe we shall and maybe not," Pitamakan replied. "It is not likely that those hunters will go home without trying to take our scalps with them; we'll soon know about that.

We watched the men in silence for some little time. Four of them were round one deer, and three were at work skinning the other. Soon, however, one man left each group and began cutting willows. Soon afterward we saw that those remaining had got the deer hides off and were cutting them into strips.

"I thought that they would do that," said my partner. "They are going to make snowshoes and follow us. Hurry now, and fasten on your shoes!"

I did as I was told and asked no questions. Pitamakan limped badly when he started off, but made light of his lameness and insisted that he felt no pain. By this time the sun was fast weakening the crust; in a short time neither we nor our enemy would be able to travel, and I told my partner that while they were making their shoes, we ought to get so far ahead that they never would be able to overtake us.

"They are seven, we only two," he said. "They will break trail by turns when the snow gets soft. Our chance to escape is to get back to the dry prairie while they are climbing the mountain on our trail."

That was a plan that had never entered my head, but I instantly saw its possibilities. Left to my own resources, I should only have struggled on and on into the mountains, eventually to be captured.

For an hour or more, just as long as the crust would hold, we kept along the side of the mountain parallel with the river; then, when the crust at last broke with us at every step, we took off our snowshoes and floundered down the tremendously steep slope to the stream, and turning with it, walked and ran along the gravelly and sandy shore.

So, not later than mid-afternoon, we came again to the foot of the mountain, and walking to the edge of the timber bordering the river, looked out on the prairie from which we had been driven in the morning.

"*Sum-is! Sum-is!*" Pitamakan cried, pointing away south to the place of the deer chase.

"*I-kit-si-kum! Sap-un-is-tsim!*" (Seven! The whole number!) I exclaimed. The horses of the enemy were picketed out there and quietly grazing, but not one of the hunters was to be seen. It seemed too good to be true.

We stood still for some time, while we searched the prairie and the mountain-side for sign of the enemy.

"They seem all to have taken our trail," said Pitamakan, at last, "and maybe that is the way of it. If one has remained to watch the horses, he must be lying in that little pine grove near them. Let's go down the river a little farther, then swing round and sneak into the grove from the other side."

We hurried on in the river-bottom for half a mile, and then swung out across the open ground. Our hearts throbbed with hope, and with fear, too, as we approached the one place where a guard might be stationed.

Stealing into the little grove as silently as shadows, we moved through it so slowly that a red squirrel digging in the needle-covered earth near by never noted our passing. There was not more than an acre of the young trees, and they covered a space twice as long as wide, so we were able to see every foot of it as we passed along. When we were nearing the farther end, a coyote gave us a terrible scare; as he rose up behind a thin screen of low boughs, we could not see at first just what it was.

I have heard of people turning cold from fear; maybe they do, but fear does not affect me in that way. A flash of heat swept through me; my mouth grew dry. My sense of being perfectly helpless, my expectation that a bullet would come tearing into me, was something that I shall never forget.

This time the suspense was short; the coyote walked boldly off in the direction in which we were going, and since the wind was in our faces, we instantly realized that no man was concealed out there ahead of him. Still, Pitamakan was cautious and, in spite of my urgent signs, kept on as stealthily as before. But when we came to the edge of the grove, we saw the coyote was walking jauntily round among the feeding horses.

Off to the right, near one of the deer carcasses, lay the hunters' saddles, saddle-blankets and other stuff. We found also a litter of willow cuttings and short strips of deer hide where the hunters had made their snowshoes. The saddles were all home-made, but better than none. We each selected one and the best of the blankets, and began saddling the two most sturdy and swift-looking of the seven animals. That done, we turned the remaining five loose, after removing their lariats and throwing them away. Then we got into the saddle and started to gather up the loose stock, when I suddenly thought of something that we had entirely forgotten in our excitement.

"Pitamakan! Our furs! Where can they be?" I asked.

"There! There!" he answered, pointing to where the other deer carcass lay.

And sure enough, there the two packs were, just as we had bound them.

Here was more luck! We lost no time in riding over to the place and picking them up; then, driving the other horses ahead of us, we rode away to the southwest as fast as possible. Somewhere on the big, timbered mountain behind us, the enemy were worming along on our trail; or, what is more likely, completely exhausted from struggling in the soft snow, they were waiting for the night freeze, to enable them to go on.

The loose horses trotted ahead of us most willingly—suspiciously so; and in the course of half an hour, on our coming to a strip of timber, the reason for such unusual conduct was plain. Here was a broad, hard trail that led, no doubt, directly to the camp which they had come from in the morning. Of course they were willing to be driven back to their mates! And now, as we pushed along this highway, one and another of them began to nicker, a sure sign that the camp was not far distant.

There were only three or four hundred yards of the timber, and then another big prairie; and at the farther end of this, a couple of miles away, smoke was rising from another patch of timber, near which many horses were grazing.

"There! There is the camp of the enemy!" Pitamakan cried. "Already they may have seen us! Let 's get back into the timber as quick as we can."

That was not easy to do; the loose stock wanted to keep right on toward their mates, and it required hard riding to head them off and turn them back. And then when we did accomplish it, they were very restless; it was only by the greatest vigilance that we kept them from breaking back.

While the sun slowly sank toward the horizon, we waited in suspense, for there was a chance that the party of seven, or some other party, might appear at any moment. The thought that, after our great success of the day, we might lose everything, and our lives also, kept us keyed up to an intense pitch of excitement.

Toward sunset there was a commotion among the horse herds at the farther end of the prairie, and two riders came loping straight toward us. At first we were not much alarmed, for we thought that they were only looking for some stray animal from the bands; but they kept coming straight on, looking neither to the right nor to the left, and it was soon plain, either that they had seen us and were going to have a look at our outfit, or that they were going to take the trail through the timber, in search, probably, of the missing hunters whose horses we had rounded up. There was but one thing for us to do — hustle the animals as far from the trail as possible; and going at it in a whirl of excitement, we hissed at them, flicked them with our bridle-ropes, and struck them with dead limbs that we snatched from the trees.

Never were horses so obstinate; they simply ducked their heads to the missiles and milled round and round among the trees and underbrush. We had got them no more than a bow-shot away from the trail, when, looking out into the open, we saw that the riders had almost reached the thin belt of timber that screened us.

"Get off your horse and try to hold him

still there behind that brush!" my partner called out; and off I slid and grasped the animal by the nose and one ear.

We could plainly hear now the thud of the oncoming horses. If one of the seven animals we had should nicker, we were lost. Presently the two riders entered the timber, and we could see them plainly as they sped along the trail. Tall, heavy men they were, with long, flying hair and grim faces. Each carried a long gun.

When they came in sight, my animal pricked up his ears and began to prance and toss his head, but I hung to him desperately, although I was hoisted more than once clear off the ground. As I swung and bobbed in the air, I got flashing glimpses of the enemy, of Pitamakan struggling with his animal, and of the loose stock looking curiously at the scene. I expected every instant that one of them would whinny, but not one of them did!

The two men passed swiftly along the trail

out of sight, and the beat of their horses' hoofs died slowly away. Then once more we took hope.

The sun was down and darkness was stealing over the land. Faint from this last narrow escape, we got into the saddle once more, and leaving the loose stock to stray whither they would, rode out into the open and took a course down the prairie that would leave the big camp far to our right. Passing it a little later, we could see the dim, yellow glow of the lodge fires, and hear the people singing, and the dogs barking now and then in answer to the mocking yelps of the coyotes.

We traveled on through the night in a partly timbered country, and, by God's mercy, safely forded some streams that were raging spring torrents. It was between midnight and dawn that we finally gave out, and, picketing our animals, lay down and slept. But the first peep of the sun roused us. Staggering to our feet, stiff and sore, we saddled, and rode on again in a half stupor. It was past noon when, from the edge of a sloping plain, we saw the big lake of the Flatheads. Pitamakan knew the place at once.

"Down there by the shore was the big camp the time we were here," he said, "and over there by the side of that little river runs the trail to buffalo land."

We came to it a little later, a broad, well-worn trail that had been used for countless years for summer travel by the mountain tribes. There were no tracks in it now save those of the wolf and the deer. Dismounting beside it to rest the horses, we took a few bites of dry meat, while they greedily cropped the tender spring grass.

We did not remain there long. Behind us stretched the trail of our horses, plain enough in the young green grass, a trail that could be easily followed from where we had first taken the animals. We went on all through the afternoon eastward into the mountains. Here the mountains were low, and in the still lower pass there was no snow to block us. Indeed, Two Medicine Pass is so low that you cannot tell when you pass the summit except by the changed course of the streamlets.

Late the next afternoon we caught a glimpse of the great plains, stretching green from the foot of the mountains away eastward to the far horizon; and at sight of them we both shouted, and Pitamakan gave thanks to his gods. Down at the foot of the mountains we saw a little later four buffalo bulls, and gave greeting to them as if they were our brothers. But not appreciating our feelings, they ran lumbering away.

Two days afterward we came to the edge of the hill overlooking Fort Benton and the Missouri, our stream of streams. The sight of it, and of our own people walking here and there outside the fort and along the river, brought tears to our eyes and great joy and peace to our hearts.

We urged our weary horses down the hill and across the bottom. An Indian boy, hunting horses, met us while we were yet some distance out, gave one look at our faces, and fled straight to the Blackfeet camp by the fort.

The people instantly poured out of the lodges and came running to greet us. Surrounded by several hundred of them, all talking at once and asking a thousand questions, we rode into the great courtyard. There, foremost of the company folk who came out to see what was the cause of all the noise, were my uncle and his wife.

They fairly tore me from my horse, smothered and crushed me with kisses and embraces, and were for leading me straight to our quarters; but I would not budge an inch until I had secured my precious pack of furs from the saddle and had given the worn animal into the keeping of one of Pitamakan's relatives.

By that time the factor himself had come from his office, and I had then and there to tell the story of our winter and our hardships in the great mountains. How the people hung upon my words, how they applauded and cheered! Without doubt those were the proudest moments of my life. For a mere boy to hold those seasoned old voyageurs and plainsmen spellbound was something of a feat, you may be sure.

But at last it was all over, and once more I entered our little house and sat down on my own soft couch of buffalo-robes. As the evening was chilly, a cheerful fire was blazing in the hearth. Tsis-tsak-ki bustled round, and while cooking the supper, managed to get out clean clothes for me, and get ready a tub of water, soap, and towels. Never before had I seen my Uncle Wesley so excited; he could not sit still. Every few moments he would come over and pinch my arm, or slap me on my back, just to make sure, as he explained, that I was really with them once more.

So ended my first great adventure on the frontier that was, and is no more.

THE END